So you really want to learn

Spanish

BOOK 2

Teacher's Book

So you really want to learn

Spanish

BOOK 2

Teacher's Book

Simon Craft M.A. (Oxon.), PGCE (Bristol)
Series Editor: Nicholas Oulton M.A. (Oxon.)

GALORE PARK

Published by Galore Park Publishing Ltd,
PO Box 96, Cranbrook, Kent TN17 4WS

Text copyright © Simon Craft 2004
Printed and bound by The Bath Press

ISBN 1 902984 27 7

All rights reserved: no part of this publication may be reproduced, stored in a retrieval system, or transmitted in any form or by any means, electronic, mechanical, photocopying, recording or otherwise, without either the prior written consent of the copyright owner or a licence permitting restricted copying issued by the Copyright Licensing Agency, 90 Tottenham Court Road, London W1P 0LP.

First published 2004

Available in the series:

So you really want to learn Spanish Book 1
    Pupil's Book   1902984102
    Teacher's book   1902984137
    Audio CD set   1902984250

So you really want to learn Spanish Book 2
    Pupil's Book   1902984269
    Teacher's book   1902984277
    Audio CD set   1902984285

So you really want to learn Spanish Book 3
    Pupil's Book   1902984307
    Teacher's book   1902984390
    Audio CD set   1902984404

Acknowledgements

The publishers would like to thank the many generous people, without whose help the production of this book, and the CD that accompanies it, would have been impossible. In particular they would like to thank Cinta Romero for her tireless work in proof-reading and checking the answers to all the exercises.

Contents

Unit 1 1
Unit 2 18
Unit 3 39
Unit 4 54
Unit 5 69
Unit 6 86

Unit 1

About the unit
In this first unit pupils will learn to describe, comprehend and compare personal characteristics. They will learn how to make simple introductions and to express thanks and appreciation.

New language content:
- use of *poco* as both an adjective and adverb
- comparative and superlative adjectives
- formation of adverbs
- direct object pronouns e.g. *lo, la, los, las*

New contexts:
- character descriptions
- meeting people, formally and informally
- being and welcoming a guest
- expressing thanks in speech and in an informal letter

Expectations

At the end of this unit most pupils will be able to: understand more detailed spoken and written descriptions of people and make comparisons between people and things; describe themselves and other people, including personal characteristics, in both speech and writing; use a range of language, including quantifiers such as *poco, bastante* to modify their descriptions; respond appropriately in different social situations such as being a guest in a Spanish-speaking family or responding to the receipt of an invitation or gift.

They should also be able to: use a wider range of language in descriptions; write extended descriptions of people and places and say why they like or dislike them.

Exercise 1.1
CD 1, track 1:

Transcript: Hola, me llamo Pepe. Tengo dieciocho años y soy de Granada. Soy andaluz. Mis padres son de Galicia, pero viven aquí desde hace veinte años a causa del trabajo de mi padre. Mi padre tiene cuarenta y cinco años y es abogado. Mi madre tiene cuarenta y dos años y es ama de casa. Solamente tengo una hermana, Yolanda, que tiene quince años. Como a ella le gusta el "Barcelona" y a mí el "Real Madrid", nos llevamos fatal. Mis padres tienen muchos hermanos y tengo un montón de primos. Soy alto, tengo el pelo moreno y, puesto que me gustan mucho las hamburguesas, estoy bastante gordo. Me gusta muchísimo el fútbol, pero mis estudios me gustan poco. En ese sentido, supongo que soy un chico bastante normal.

Translation: Hello, my name's Pepe. I'm eighteen and from Granada. I'm from Andalucia. My parents are from Galicia, but they've lived here for twenty years because of my father's work. My father's forty-five and he's a lawyer. My mother's forty-two and she's a housewife. I only have one sister, Yolanda, who's fifteen. As she likes Barcelona and I like Real Madrid, we don't get on at all. My parents have lots of siblings and I've got loads of cousins. I'm tall with dark hair, and because I really like hamburgers, I'm pretty fat. I love football, but don't like studying very much at all. In this way, I suppose I'm quite a normal boy.

Suggestions: Pupils should be encouraged to take notes as specified in the pupils' book. The following questions should be asked by the teacher afterwards.

Answers:
1. *Se llama Pepe.*
2. *Tiene 18 años.*
3. *Son de Galicia. Viven en Granada desde hace 20 años. El padre de Pepe tiene 45 años y es abogado. La madre tiene 42 años y es ama de casa.*
4. *Se lleva fatal porque a él le gusta el Real Madrid y a ella el Barcelona.*
5. *Le gustan las hamburguesas y le gusta el fútbol.*
6. *Es alto con el pelo moreno y está bastante gordo.*

Exercise 1.2

Suggestions: Pupils should be asked to read out some of their versions in turn, and the rest told to make notes in order to be prepared to answer questions afterwards. Pupils could then be asked to make a list of any further adjectives they can recall – these can be identified afterwards. Also, pupils could be asked to make a list of adjectives that are similar in English, e.g. *sociable, agresivo* etc.

Exercise 1.3
Answers:
1. *Mi suegra **es guapa**.*
2. *Su nieto **tiene** los ojos **azules**.*
3. *Sus hijas **son inteligentes**.*
4. *Yo **tengo** una camisa **negra**.*
5. *Nosotros **estamos cansados**.*

Translations:
1. My mother-in-law is pretty.
2. His grandson has blue eyes.
3. His daughters are intelligent.
4. I have a black shirt.
5. We are tired.

Suggestions: Pupils could be asked to invent their own sentences using the format above. They could be told to use different parts of *tener, ser, estar* and to use some of the adjectives that have recently been covered. In particular, it would seem sensible if these sentences could relate to personal descriptions in some way, as in numbers 1 and 2 above. These sentences could then be read out and used as additional listening and speaking work.

Exercise 1.4

The passage may be listened to while pupils read it in their books.

CD 1, track 2:

Ramón:	*Hola. Yo me llamo Ramón, ¿y tú?*
Paco:	*Yo soy Francisco, pero todo el mundo me llama Paco. Encantado de conocerte.*
Ramón:	*Igualmente. ¿Tienes muchos hermanos?*
Paco:	*Bueno, tengo dos hermanos y una hermana. ¿Y tú?*
Ramón:	*Yo tengo una hermana.*
Paco:	*¿Te llevas bien con ella?*
Ramón:	*Sí, porque siempre me presenta a todas sus amigas guapas.*
Paco:	*¡Qué suerte! Yo me llevo fatal con la mía. Es muy antipática.*
Ramón:	*¿Por qué?*
Paco:	*Porque nunca me deja ver el fútbol. Es que es mayor que yo y siempre quiere ver 'Operación Triunfo'.*
Ramón:	*¿Qué es eso?*
Paco:	*¿Realmente no lo sabes? Es un programa de música.*
Ramón:	*Es que nosotros no tenemos televisión en casa.*
Paco:	*¡Qué raro! De todas formas me gustaría ir a tu casa. Tu hermana parece ser mucho más simpática que la mía.*
Ramón:	*Bueno. Puedes venir esta noche si quieres.*
Paco:	*¡Estupendo!*

Translation:

Ramón:	Hello. My name's Ramón, and yours?
Paco:	My name's Francisco, but everyone calls me Paco. Pleased to meet you.
Ramón:	Me too. Do you have lots of brothers and sisters?
Paco:	Well, I've got two brothers and one sister. And you?
Ramón:	I have a sister.
Paco:	Do you get on well with her?
Ramón:	Yes as she always introduces me to her good-looking friends.
Paco:	You're so lucky. I get on terribly with mine. She's really unpleasant.
Ramón:	Why?
Paco:	She never lets me watch the football. The thing is she's older than me and she always wants to watch *Operación Triunfo*.
Ramón:	What's that?
Paco:	You really don't know? It's a music programme.
Ramón:	We don't have a television at home.
Paco:	How odd! Regardless, I'd still like to go to your house. Your sister seems a good deal nicer than mine.
Ramón:	Fine. You can come round this evening if you want.
Paco:	Fantastic.

Answers to questions:
1. *Paco, porque Ramón solamente tiene una hermana.*
2. *Ramón, porque le presenta a todas sus amigas guapas.*
3. *Porque no le deja su hermana.*
4. *Esta noche.*

Translations:
1. Paco, because Ramón only has one sister.
2. Ramón, because she introduces him to all her good-looking friends.
3. Because his sister doesn't let him.
4. This evening.

Suggestions: You could now get the pupils to split into pairs and invent a conversation between two young people meeting for the first time. They could be told they must mention age, family, including family character description, as well as incorporating at least one use of the comparative adjective. Pupils could then enact their conversations in turn, the rest being asked to take notes with a view to answering questions afterwards.

Exercise 1.5

Suggestions: While pupils are inventing sentences with the comparative and superlative, you could wander round correcting or helping as required. After a sufficient time, pupils should be encouraged to read out some examples. These could be written down spontaneously on the OHP/board and analysed with the class for errors. Alternatively, the teacher could enhance pupils' command of this issue by getting pupils to repeat what has just been said. Another pupil could be chosen to translate. This helps to make sure pupils know they have to maintain concentration.

Exercise 1.6
CD 1, track 3:

Transcript:
Elena:	*Hola, ¿qué tal? Yo soy Elena. Soy de aquí, de Granada.*
Angela:	*Hola, yo me llamo Angela. Soy de Londres.*
Elena:	*Me gustaría muchísimo conocer Londres. ¿Cómo es?*
Angela:	*Está bien, pero me gusta más Granada.*
Elena:	*¿Por qué?*
Angela:	*Granada es más tranquila que Londres. La gente es más relajada. Además, Londres tiene que ser la ciudad más sucia del mundo. Y la menos segura. Los chicos no son tan guapos, pero ningún sitio es perfecto.*
Elena:	*Yo viajo muy poco, entonces no conozco muchos países. De todas formas, me extraña lo que dices sobre Londres. Todos mis amigos piensan que Granada es la ciudad más ruidosa y sucia del planeta.*
Angela:	*¡Qué va! Granada es una maravilla.*

Translation:
Elena:	Hi, how are you? I'm Elena. I'm from here, from Granada.
Angela:	Hi, I'm Angela. I'm from London.
Elena:	I'd really like to know London. What's it like?
Angela:	It's fine, but I prefer Granada.
Elena:	Why?
Angela:	Granada is quieter than London. The people are more relaxed. Besides, London's got to be the dirtiest city in the world. And the least safe. The boys aren't so good-looking here, but nowhere's perfect.

Elena:	I travel very little, so I don't know many countries. At any rate, I'm surprised by what you say about London. All my friends think that Granada is the noisiest and dirtiest city on the planet.
Angela:	No way! Granada's fantastic.

Answers to questions:
1. Elena es española y Angela es inglesa.
2. Dice que es más tranquila y que la gente es más relajada.
3. Los chicos no son tan guapos como en Londres.
4. Sus amigos piensan que Granada es la ciudad más ruidosa y sucia del mundo, pero no lo es.

Translations:
1. Elena is Spanish and Angela is English.
2. She says it's quieter and the people are more relaxed.
3. The boys are not as good-looking as in London.
4. Her friends think that Granada is the noisiest and dirtiest city in the world, but it isn't.

Exercise 1.7

Suggestions: Before initiating this exercise, you should anticipate any vocabulary problems the pupils might have and should therefore make sure they know all the appropriate words to describe the people in the photos, e.g tall, thin, fat, good-looking etc. The exercise above could incorporate use of the superlative, e.g. *Juanjo es el chico más guapo.* As usual, it is sensible to get pupils to read out examples, and then to ask others what has been said. As homework, pupils could be asked to invent 10 further sentences, 5 using the comparative and 5 using the superlative. In order to stretch their vocabulary, they should be encouraged to find and use different adjectives from the ones that they have used for Exercise 1.7.

Exercise 1.8

CD1: 4

Pupils should be clear about the meaning of the words to be inserted as well as those in the text before beginning the exercise. A recording of the passage is available on the CD: CD 1, track 4.

CD 1, track 4:

Transcript (answers to exercise in bold):

Paco:	Oye, Julio, ¿por qué no compras el pan hoy?
Julio:	Pero tú has dormido mucho más que yo, y yo **estoy** mucho **más cansado** que tú.
Paco:	Mira, yo soy **mayor** que tú, y tienes que obedecerme.
Julio:	Pero eso es **muy** injusto. Eres un **egoísta**.
Paco:	Lo **siento**. El **mundo** es así.
Julio:	Y otra cosa. Me debes **diez** euros.
Paco:	Si eres **más generoso** que yo, ése no **es** mi problema.

Translation of exercise:

Paco:	Listen, Julio, why don't you buy the bread today?
Julio:	But you've slept much more than me and I'm a lot more tired than you.
Paco:	Look, I'm older than you and you have to obey me.
Julio:	But that's really unfair. You're a selfish person.
Paco:	I'm sorry. That's the way the world is.
Julio:	And another thing. You owe me 10 euros.
Paco:	If you're more generous than me, that's not my problem.

Exercise 1.9

Answers to exercise:
1. *Paco es más egoísta que Julio.*
2. *Paco es mayor que Julio.*
3. *Julio es más generoso que Paco.*
4. *Julio es menor que Paco.*

Translations:
1. Paco is more selfish than Julio.
2. Paco is older than Julio.
3. Julio is more generous than Paco.
4. Julio is younger than Paco.

Translation of letter:

Dear María,

Hi. How's it going? My name's Julia. I'm English, I'm fifteen years old, and I'm the daughter of some friends of your parents. The fact is I'm really interested in doing an exchange with a boy or girl my age. Why don't I describe what I'm like and what I do and don't like and then we can see whether we have the same things in common? I'm pretty tall with blond hair and blue eyes. How about you? I live with my parents and my brother Fabian in a pretty big house on the outskirts of London. Where do you live and what do you think of it? How do you get on with your family? I get on really well with my parents because they're very tolerant, but I get on terribly with Fabian. He's much more intelligent than me, but a good deal more unfriendly. If you have brothers and sisters, what are they like? I love going to the cinema and going out with my friends on the weekends. I'm not very sporty, but I like skiing. I really like travelling and my favourite country is Spain which I know well as my mother is from Seville. I'm mad about soap operas on television. I love buying clothes and music, but I don't like having to go to the supermarket with my mother to do the shopping. Neither do I enjoy having to go on holiday with my brother. What a nightmare! Tell me what you like doing and what you don't. What's your favourite country?

Well, I really want to get to know more about you. Try to reply soon.

Love,

Julia

Suggestions: It is obviously important that pupils understand the text completely before writing their own letter. When this happens they should be encouraged to use useful vocabulary within the original letter, e.g. *me encanta* + infinitive *or no me gusta* + infinitive.

The letter also contains some fundamental aspects of grammar. This could provide a good opportunity to revise or indeed initiate analysis of pronouns, and verbs such as *gustar*. If appropriate, the text could be used for additional tasks such as identifying all the direct/indirect object pronouns in the text and revising the rules as regards their location.

UNIT 1: ¡Hola!

Exercise 1.11
CD 1, track 5:

Transcript:

Carlos: *Hola, me llamo Carlos y tengo dieciséis años. Soy de Bilbao, pero llevo cuatro años viviendo en Valencia. Me gusta mucho más el clima aquí, pero echo mucho de menos a mis amigos y a mis primos. Soy bastante alto – mido un metro noventa – y yo creo que soy delgado, pero mi madre me regaña porque dice que estoy todo el día comiendo galletas y patatas fritas y que me voy a poner gordísimo. Yo creo que ella es muy exagerada. Mi padre es mucho más tranquilo que mi madre. Es muy tolerante y por eso me llevo tan bien con él. Tengo un hermano, Manolo, que tiene dieciocho años y nos entendemos bastante bien. A los dos nos gustan los deportes, sobre todo el fútbol y el baloncesto. También me gusta mucho el ciclismo.*

Intento ir mucho al cine. Me interesan mucho las películas extranjeras, menos las de Hollywood que me aburren mucho. No me gusta mucho leer, salvo los periódicos deportivos como el "Marca". Tampoco me gusta demasiado el instituto, pero el inglés se me da bastante bien y el profesor es muy entretenido. Viajo poco y me gustaría conocer Inglaterra, no solamente Londres sino el campo también; dicen que es precioso.

Translation:

Carlos: Hi, my name's Carlos and I'm sixteen. I'm from Bilbao, but I've been living in Valencia for four years. I far prefer the climate here, but I really miss my friends and cousins. I'm pretty tall – 1 metre and 90 centimetres – and I think I'm thin, but my mother tells me off because she says I spend the whole time eating biscuits and crisps and that I'm going to get really fat. I think she goes way over the top. My father is much more easy-going than my mother. He's very tolerant and that's why we get on so well. I have a brother Manolo who's eighteen and we get on pretty well. We both like sport, especially football and basketball. I also really like cycling. I try to go to the cinema very often. I like foreign films, not the usual Hollywood fare which I find boring. I don't really like reading unless it's a sports newspaper like "*Marca*". Neither am I particularly fond of school, but I'm pretty good at English and the teacher is very entertaining. I don't travel a great deal and I would like to visit England, not only London, but the countryside too; they tell me it's beautiful.

The tape should be played at least twice, allowing the pupils the opportunity to take notes and possibly spell out words which they do not recognise, but which could be clarified later by the teacher. The following questions should be posed for each of the 3 individuals:

1. *¿Dónde vive?*
2. *¿Cómo es físicamente?*
3. *¿Cómo se lleva con sus padres?*
4. *¿Qué pasatiempos tiene?*
5. *¿Qué dice de su instituto?*
6. *¿Qué dice sobre viajar?*

If appropriate, more questions could be asked.

Answers for Carlos:
1. *Vive en Valencia.*
2. *Es bastante alto y delgado.*
3. *Se lleva bien con su padre, pero no tan bien con su madre.*
4. *Le gusta el deporte, sobre todo el fútbol, el baloncesto y el ciclismo. Le gustan también las películas extranjeras.*
5. *No le gusta mucho, pero le gustan las clases de inglés.*
6. *No viaja mucho; le gustaría conocer Inglaterra.*

The teacher could also go through all the useful vocabulary, asking pupils to write it down and to learn for homework. A test could be performed at the beginning of the next lesson. Alternatively, pupils could be asked to provide a written description of themselves using the same format as that used by Carlos. This could be done either in class (with people reading out examples) or as homework.

CD 1, track 6:

Transcript:

María: *Hola, yo me llamo María. Tengo quince años y soy de Granada. Soy bastante baja, con los ojos negros. Soy morena y tengo el pelo liso y muy largo. Mis amigas me dicen que soy muy guapa, pero yo no estoy tan segura. No me gustan nada los deportes. Me aburren muchísimo. Yo prefiero ver las telenovelas en la televisión. Me encantan. Me gusta bastante el instituto; los profesores son simpáticos y tengo muchos amigos. Claro, no me gusta mucho tener que hacer los deberes, pero así es la vida. Soy bastante marchosa, así que me gusta mucho salir. También me encanta ir de compras. A mi novio no le gusta nada esto porque dice que paso más tiempo en las tiendas que con él. Tampoco les gusta a mis padres porque dicen que gasto demasiado dinero. Me encanta la música. Sobre todo me gusta Miguel Bosé. Mis amigas dicen que ya está muy viejo, pero a mí me gusta. He viajado mucho y hay varios países que me gustan, pero me encanta España. Aquí hay de todo – playa, montaña, campo. Incluso se puede esquiar. Aquí en Granada hay una estación de esquí maravillosa – se llama Sierra Nevada. Sería muy difícil para mí vivir en otro sitio, pero me encantaría poder volver a Inglaterra.*

Translation: Hi, my name's María. I'm fifteen and I'm from Granada. I'm quite short with dark eyes. My hair's dark and is straight and very long. My friends tell me I'm very pretty, but I'm not so sure. I can't stand sports. I find them really boring. I far prefer watching soap operas on television. I love them. I quite like school; the teachers are nice and I've got lots of friends there. Obviously, I'm not very keen on doing my homework, but such is life. I'm quite outward-going and so I like to go out a lot. I also love going shopping. My boyfriend doesn't like this at all as he says I spend more time in the shops than I do with him. My parents aren't too keen either as they say I spend too much money. I love music, especially *Miguel Bosé*. My friends say he's really old now, but I like him. I've travelled quite extensively and there are lots of countries I like, but I still love Spain. There's everything you want here – beaches, mountains, countryside. You can even go skiing here. There's a wonderful ski resort here in Granada – it's called the *Sierra Nevada*. It would be really difficult for me to live anywhere else, but I would love to be able to go back to England.

Questions:
1. *¿Dónde vive?*
2. *¿Cómo es físicamente?*
3. *¿Cómo se lleva con sus padres?*
4. *¿Qué pasatiempos tiene?*
5. *¿Qué dice de su instituto?*
6 *¿Qué dice sobre viajar?*

Answers for María:
1. *Vive en Granada.*
2. *Es baja, morena, con el pelo liso y muy largo; es muy guapa.*
3. *No habla de sus padres.*
4. *Le gusta salir y le encanta ir de compras. Le gusta mucho la música.*
5. *Le gusta bastante. Los profesores son simpáticos y tiene muchos amigos.*
6. *Le gusta. Conoce varios países.*

UNIT 1: ¡Hola!

CD 1, track 7:

Transcript:

Jorge: *Hola, mi nombre verdadero es Jorge, pero casi todo el mundo me llama El Gordo puesto que me encanta comer. Me lo como todo – carne, pescado, "chuches", todo menos fruta – la fruta no me gusta en absoluto. Como te puedes imaginar soy un poco gordo, pero soy simpático, creo, y tengo un montón de amigos. Vivo en un pueblo cerca de Sevilla. Tengo bastantes aficiones. Sobre todo me gusta el toreo. Mi torero favorito es El Juli; es muy valiente. Quiero verlo torear este año en La Maestranza, la plaza de toros de Sevilla. Va a ser genial. También me gustan los coches. En cuanto me saque el carné el año que viene, me voy a comprar uno y voy a ir en coche a Santander para ver a mis primos que viven allí. Son once y nos llevamos fenomenal. También tengo muchas ganas de ir porque se come muy bien allí y la sidra está muy buena. Además, puedo escaparme de mis padres. No nos llevamos muy bien porque siempre me están diciendo que no coma tanto.*

Translation:
Hi, my real name is Jorge, but virtually everyone calls me *El Gordo* (The Fat One) as I absolutely love eating. I eat anything – meat, fish, sweets, everything except fruit, which I can't stand. As you can probably imagine, I'm a little bit on the fat side, but I'm a nice guy, I think, and I've got lots of friends. I live in a village near Sevilla. I have a number of interests. Above all, I like bullfighting. My favourite bullfighter is El Juli; he's really brave. I want to see him fight this year at La Maestranza, the bullring in Sevilla. It will be awesome. I also love cars. As soon as I get my licence I'm going to drive to Santander to see my cousins who live there. There are eleven of them and we get on really well. I'm also really keen as the food is great there and they have really good cider. I can also get away from my parents. We don't get on too well because they always tell me not to eat so much.

Questions:
1. ¿Dónde vive?
2. ¿Cómo es físicamente?
3. ¿Cómo se lleva con sus padres?
4. ¿Qué pasatiempos tiene?
5. ¿Qué dice de su colegio?
6. ¿Qué dice sobre viajar?

Answers for Jorge:
1. Vive en un pueblo cerca de Sevilla.
2. Es un poco gordo, pero muy simpático.
3. No se lleva bien con ellos.
4. Le gusta el toreo.
5. No habla de su colegio.
6. Quiere ir a Santander para ver a sus primos.

Exercise 1.12

Suggestions: Pupils should be encouraged to read out their accounts while the others take notes in preparation for oral questions afterwards.

Sample answer:
Yo prefiero a Jorge. Es simpático y tiene muchos amigos. Le gusta mucho comer y a mí también me gusta comer. Le gusta el toreo y yo creo que es un espectáculo interesante. Le gustan los coches, y a mí también me gustan.

Exercise 1.13

Suggestions: CD 1 Tracks 5-7 should be played again, preferably only once as pupils have already heard this information. Pupils should listen for and be asked to read out examples of the use of *gustar* and *encantar*. It is important to reinforce exactly how the verbs work when followed both by nouns and verbs. As far as the latter is concerned, a common mistake is to use *gustar* with a gerund (translating literally from the English) when, of course, an infinitive is required, e.g. *me gusta **jugar** al fútbol*). If possible, it would also be valuable to show how these verbs are governed by the pronouns *me, te, le, nos, os, les*.

Answers:
1. Carlos:
   Me gusta mucho más el clima aquí.
   A los dos nos gustan los deportes.
   Me gusta mucho el ciclismo.
   No me gusta mucho leer.
   Tampoco me gusta demasiado el instituto.
   Me gustaría conocer Inglaterra.

2. María:
   No me gustan nada los deportes.
   (Las telenovelas) me encantan.
   Me gusta bastante el instituto.
   No me gusta mucho tener que hacer los deberes.
   Me gusta mucho salir.
   Me encanta ir de compras.
   A mi novio no le gusta nada esto.
   Tampoco les gusta a mis padres.
   Me encanta la música
   Me gusta Miguel Bosé.
   A mí me gusta.
   Hay varios países que me gustan.
   Me encanta España
   Me encantaría poder volver a Inglaterra.

3. Jorge:
   Me encanta comer.
   La fruta no me gusta en absoluto.
   Me gusta el toreo.
   Me gustan los coches.

Exercise 1.14

Answers to exercise:
1. *Me gusta salir con mis amigos.*
2. *Le encanta comer.*
3. *Le gusta esquiar y viajar.*
4. *¿Te gustan las hamburguesas?*
5. *Le gustan los deportes.*

Exercise 1.15
Answers to task:
1. rápidamente
2. lentamente
3. locamente
4. tristemente
5. felizmente

Homework: Pupils should be asked to revise the vocabulary list with a view to doing a test next lesson.

Exercise 1.16
Suggestions: Having verified the correct forms of the adverbs above, individual pupils could be asked to read out examples of their sentences and others asked to repeat what has been said. Pupils could then be asked to create more sentences using adverbs other than the ones above.

Exercise 1.17
A recording of the completed passage is available on the CD.

CD 1, track 8:
Answers to task (in bold):
Julio está muy enfadado con su hermano y sale de su dormitorio **furiosamente**. Pero ya son las nueve y media y **normalmente** desayunan a las nueve. Tiene mucha prisa y entonces va **rápidamente** a la panadería. Pero el panadero ya es muy viejo y trabaja bastante **lentamente**. Ya es tarde. Julio mira su reloj **nerviosamente**. Sus padres van a estar muy enfadados. **Finalmente** le atiende el panadero. Cuando llega Julio a casa son las diez y cuarto. ¿Dónde demonios has estado? le pregunta **furiosamente** su padre.

Translation:
Julio is very angry with his brother and goes **furiously** out of his bedroom. But by now it is half-past nine and they **normally** have breakfast at nine. He is in a real hurry and so he goes **quickly** to the baker's. But the baker is now an old man and he works pretty **slowly**. It is now late. Julio looks at his watch **nervously**. His parents are going to be really angry. **Eventually** the baker serves him. When Julio arrives home it is quarter past ten. 'Where on earth have you been?' his father asks him **furiously**.

Exercise 1.18
Suggestions: While pupils are doing this task, it would be sensible to wander round the class checking their work and helping them with vocabulary and grammar. When they have finished, some pupils could read out their stories, while the others listen and make notes in preparation for questions in Spanish afterwards. Alternatively, this exercise could be set for homework.

So you really want to learn Spanish – Teacher's Book

Exercise 1.19

A recording of the passage is available on the CD.

CD 1, track 9:

Transcript (with pronouns underlined):

Carlos: *Esta noche ponen el partido entre el Betis y el Sevilla. ¿Te apetece ver<u>lo</u>?*
Manolo: *¿A qué hora <u>lo</u> ponen?*
Carlos: *A las nueve.*
Madre: *<u>Lo</u> siento. Tenemos que ir a casa de la abuela.*
Carlos: *Pero mamá, ¿otra vez?*
Madre: *¿Es que no queréis ver<u>la</u>?*
Manolo: *Claro que queremos ver<u>la</u>, pero <u>la</u> vamos a ver el domingo también.*
Madre: *¿Y los deberes, <u>los</u> habéis hecho?*
Manolo: *Yo no tengo.*
Carlos: *Voy a hacer<u>los</u> ahora mismo.*
Madre: *Bueno, pero quita la tele.*
Carlos: *Pero mamá, quiero ver 'El rival más débil'.*
Madre: *Quíta<u>la</u> te digo.*
Carlos: *Vale, vale.*

Translation:

Carlos: The Betis-Sevilla match is on TV tonight. Do you feel like watching it?
Manolo: What time's it on?
Carlos: Nine o'clock.
Mother: I'm sorry, but we've got to go and see Grandma.
Carlos: But mum, again?
Mother: What, don't you want to see her?
Manolo: Of course we want to see her, but we're going to see her on Sunday as well.
Mother: And your homework? Have you done it?
Manolo: I haven't got any.
Carlos: I'm going to do mine right away.
Mother: OK, but turn off the TV.
Carlos: But Mum, I want to watch 'The Weakest Link'.
Mother: Turn it off I said.
Carlos: OK, OK.

Exercise 1.20

Answers to exercise:
1. *Está comiéndolas/las está comiendo*
2. *¡Cómela!*
3. *Quiero verlo/lo quiero ver*
4. *Vamos a verla mañana/la vamos a ver mañana*
5. *Los ven*

Translations:
1. He is eating them.
2. Eat it!
3. I want to see it.
4. We're going to see her tomorrow.
5. They see them.

Suggestions: You would need to point out that, as numbers 1, 3 and 4 show, the pronoun can go before the principal verb.

Exercise 1.21

Suggestions: Pupils should be asked to read out examples and others asked to repeat what has been said. They could also be asked the English meaning of what has been said. This type of exercise could be extended for homework – for example, they could be asked to invent another 10 sentences. Also, an extra dimension could be added, e.g. pupils could be asked to incorporate an adverb into the sentence. For example, *Carlos los hace rápidamente.* This would reinforce the work recently done on this subject.

Exercise 1.22

Passage (with pronouns and adverbs underlined):

Granada, 3 de marzo de 2003

Querida Julia:

Muchas gracias por tu carta. La recibí ayer. ¡Qué ilusión! Obviamente, tenemos muchas cosas en común. La idea de hacer un intercambio me interesa mucho. A mí también me gustan las telenovelas. Normalmente las veo todos los días. ¿Cómo son las telenovelas allí? ¿Cuándo las ves? ¿También te gusta la música? ¿Conoces a Miguel Bosé? Si no, te lo voy a poner. Tengo todos sus discos.

Voy a hablar con mis padres sobre el intercambio. Yo creo que es una idea fantástica. Granada te va a gustar, sobre todo si te gusta esquiar. Si vienes en abril, podemos subir a la sierra y luego, si hace bueno, ir a la playa. Generalmente, yo voy todos los fines de semana. ¿Qué haces normalmente los fines de semana en Londres?

Bueno, tengo que irme porque el culebrón está a punto de empezar.

Escríbeme pronto

Un abrazo

María

Translation:

Granada, 3rd March, 2003

Dear Julia,

Many thanks for your letter. I received it yesterday. How exciting! We obviously have a lot in common. I am really interested in the idea of an exchange. I also like soap operas. Normally, I watch them every day. What are they like there? When do you watch them? You also like music? Do you know *Miguel Bosé?* If not, I'll introduce you to his music when you come. I've got all his records.

I'm going to speak to my parents about the exchange. I think it's a great idea. You'll love Granada, I'm sure, especially if you like skiing. If you come in April, we can go to the mountains and then, if the weather's good, go to the beach. Generally speaking, I go every weekend. What do you normally do at the weekends in London?

Well, I have to go as the soap's about to start.

Write soon

Love,

María

Exercise 1.24
Answers to exercise (in bold):
1. Yo **voy** a **comprar** pan
2. Mis padres **van** a **visitar** a mi abuela
3. ¿Tú **vas** a **ver** la película?
4. Jorge **va** a **comer** cinco bocadillos enormes
5. Nosotros **vamos** a **tomar** una cerveza

Translations:
1. I'm going to buy bread.
2. My parents are going to visit my grandmother.
3. Are you going to see the film?
4. Jorge is going to eat 5 enormous sandwiches.
5. We are going to have a beer.

Exercise 1.26
CD 1, track 10:
Transcript:
Madre:	Hola Julia, encantada de conocerte.
Julia:	Igualmente. ¿Cómo está usted?
Madre:	No hace falta que me hables de usted. Estoy muy bien, gracias. ¿Qué tal el viaje?
Julia:	Regular. Es que a mí no me gusta volar.
Madre:	Bueno, ya estás aquí. Tienes que tener hambre. ¿Te apetece tomar algo antes de que María te enseñe tu cuarto? ¿Te gustan los embutidos?
Julia:	¿Qué son embutidos exactamente?
Madre:	Bueno, chorizo, salchichón, jamón, cosas como ésas.
Julia:	Me apetece mucho un bocadillo de jamón. Muchas gracias.
Madre:	De nada. ¿Te pongo algo de beber?
Julia:	Sí, por favor. ¿Tiene … quiero decir tienes agua con gas?
Madre:	Claro. Y a ti, María, ¿te apetece algo?
María:	Sí, mamá. ¿Me preparas un bocata de atún?
Madre:	¿Y de beber?
María:	A mí me apetece zumo de naranja.

Translation:
Mother:	Hello, Julia. Pleased to meet you.
Julia:	Me too. How are you?
Mother:	You don't need to use *usted* with me. I'm fine, thank you. How was the journey?
Julia:	Not brilliant. I don't like flying.
Mother:	Well, you're here now. You must be hungry. Do you feel like something to eat before María shows you your room? Do you like *embutidos*?
Julia:	What are they exactly?
Mother:	Well, chorizo, salami sausage, ham, things like that.
Julia:	A ham sandwich would be great. Thanks very much.
Mother:	You're welcome. Can I fix you a drink?
Julia:	Yes please. Have you got any fizzy water?
Mother:	Of course. How about you, María? Do you feel like anything?
María:	Yes, Mum. Could you make me a tuna sandwich?
Mother:	What would you like to drink?
María:	I feel like an orange juice.

UNIT 1: ¡Hola! | 15

Answers to exercise:
1. *Dice que regular porque no le gusta volar.*
2. *Son productos como chorizo, salchichón, jamón.*
3. *A Julia le apetece un bocadillo de jamón.*
4. *María quiere un bocata de atún.*
5. *Julia quiere beber agua con gas, y María, zumo de naranja.*

Translations:
1. She says it was so-so as she doesn't like flying.
2. It means products like *chorizo*, salami-type sausage and ham.
3. She feels like a ham sandwich.
4. She wants a tuna sandwich.
5. Julia wants fizzy water, and María an orange juice.

Suggestions: There are a number of points to be picked up on after questions have been answered and gone through. For example, it is well worth reinforcing useful vocabulary in this context, e.g. *encantado/a de conocerte/lo, igualmente etc* which should be used in the next exercise. It could also provide a further opportunity to reinforce unconventional verbs like *apetecer* and *gustar*. Equally, it could naturally lead on to some vocabulary work on food and drink.

Exercise 1.27

Suggestion: Role plays should be enacted and used for oral work.

Exercise 1.28

A recording of the passage is available on the CD.

CD 1, track 11:

María:	*Bueno, Julia, ¿qué tal tu habitación, te gusta?*
Julia:	*Sí, está muy bien. Es mucho más grande que mi cuarto en Londres. Mira, te traigo un regalo.*
María:	*Muchísimas gracias. ¿Qué es?*
Julia:	*Como te gusta la música, aquí tienes un CD de "The Stone Roses".*
María:	*¿Las rosas de piedra?*
Julia:	*Sí, así es.*
María:	*Un nombre interesante. Muchas gracias. Yo también tengo un regalo para ti. Toma.*
Julia:	*Un CD de 'Operación Triunfo'. ¡Qué maravilla! Muchas gracias.*
María:	*De nada. ¿Qué te apetece hacer luego?*
Julia:	*No sé. Lo que quieras.*
María:	*¿Qué tal si salimos de tapas? ¿Te gusta tapear?*
Julia:	*Sí, mucho. Suena muy bien.*

Translation:

María:	Well, Julia, what do you think of your room? Do you like it?
Julia:	Yes, it's really nice. It's much bigger than my room in London. Look, I've brought you a present.
María:	Thanks a lot. What is it?
Julia:	Seeing as you like music, I got you a CD of 'The Stone Roses'.
María:	The Stone Roses?
Julia:	Yes, that's right.
María:	An interesting name. Thanks a lot. I got you a present too. Here you go.
Julia:	A CD of 'Operación Triunfo'. Fantastic! Thanks a lot.
María:	You're welcome. What do you feel like doing later.
Julia:	I don't know. Whatever.
María:	How about if we go and have a few *tapas*? Do you like eating *tapas*?
Julia:	Yes, very much. It sounds great.

Answers to questions:
1. *Dice que le gusta y que es mucho más grande que su habitación en Londres.*
2. *Un CD de 'Operación Triunfo'.*
3. *Luego van a salir de tapas.*

Translations:
1. She says she likes it and it's much bigger than her room in London.
2. A CD of *'Operación Triunfo'*.
3. They're going to go out for some *tapas*.

Exercise 1.29

Suggestions: It would be worth walking round the class, helping or correcting where necessary. Pupils could be asked to enact their dialogues afterwards, and the other class members could be asked questions, e.g. *¿Qué piensa el amigo de Jorge de su cuarto? ¿Qué se regalan? ¿Qué piensan de sus regalos?*

Exercise 1.30

Translation:

Dear Family Márquez

I'm writing to you to thank you for a truly wonderful stay in your house. I had a wonderful time. Many thanks for your generosity and for showing me so many beautiful places. I loved all those tapas bars, especially *La Papa* where they serve all those different potato dishes. I also really liked that bar near *Plaza Nueva* where they serve that fish which tastes so good. The prawns are incredibly tasty.

Thanks also for having taken me to *La Alhambra*. It's a truly awesome place. I especially like the gardens with all that water and so many flowers. How beautiful!

María, many thanks for the present. I love it. I'm driving my family mad as I play the *'Operación Triunfo'* CD every day. I think that they're a little fed up with *David Bisbal* by now.

The *embutidos* have also been a success. We've eaten almost all the ham and cheese. They sell that type of food here, but it's much more expensive than in Spain. My father also says thank you. He's already drunk the five bottles of red wine. We've had to buy some more aspirins as a result! My mother loves the perfume.

Well, I must go as Neighbours starts in five minutes' time and I want to grab the best armchair before my brother.

Lots of love and many thanks once again for everything.

Julia

Answers to questions:
1. *Porque ponen muchos platos diferentes de patatas.*
2. *Porque ponen un pescado muy bueno. También le gustaron las gambas.*
3. *Dice que es impresionante. Le gustó porque tiene unos jardines muy bonitos.*
4. *La familia está harta, puesto que Julia pone el disco todos los días.*
5. *Porque son más baratos.*
6. *Ninguna.*
7. *Recibió perfume.*
8. *Porque quiere sentarse en el mejor sillón para ver la telenovela.*

Translations:
1. Because they serve lots of different potato dishes.
2. Because they serve really good fish dishes.
3. She says it is fabulous. She liked it because of the beautiful gardens.
4. They're fed up with him as Julia plays the CD every day.
5. Because they're cheaper.
6. None.
7. She received perfume.
8. Because she wants to sit in the best armchair to watch the soap opera.

Suggestions: This exercise could be used to reinforce use of direct object pronouns as well as adverbs. Pupils could be asked to go back through the text underling all the different examples of pronouns and adverbs. There are several examples of *por* and this could lead to revision of the *por v para* issue. An alternative would be to focus on the use of *por* in this instance, i.e. exchange. Pupils could be asked to invent their own examples, e.g. *pagó diez libras **por** el libro.*

Exercise 1.31

Suggestions: This exercise could either be used for homework or alternatively as a task to be performed in class. In the case of the latter, individual pupils would be asked to read out what they had written and other pupils asked questions afterwards.

Summary of unit

Pupils should now be able to: understand more detailed spoken and written descriptions of people and make comparisons between people and things; describe themselves and other people, including personal characteristics, in both speech and writing; use a range of language, including quantifiers such as **poco, bastante** to modify their descriptions; respond appropriately in different social situations such as being a guest in a Spanish-speaking family or responding to the receipt of an invitation or gift.

They might also be able to: use a wider range of language in descriptions; write extended descriptions of people and places and say why they like or dislike them.

Unit 2

About the unit
In this unit pupils will learn to discuss their likes, dislikes and preferences as regards food and drink. They will also learn about quantities and be able to devise recipes.

New language content:
- direct object pronouns with things (*lo, la, los, las*)
- expressions of quantity
- using *tener hambre/sed*
- use of disjunctive pronoun with preposition, e.g. *para mí*

New contexts:
- food and drink
- likes, dislikes and preferences
- following and preparing recipes
- buying food
- restaurant/*tapas*
- Christmas food

Expectations
At the end of this unit pupils should be able to: understand spoken and written descriptions of food and recipes; state their preferences for food and drink, including cuisines from different countries; order a meal or *tapas* for themselves or others from memory, or tell someone what they would like.

They should also be able to: understand more complex spoken and written descriptions of food and recipes; state more detailed preferences for food and drink.

Exercise 2.1

Suggestions: Before beginning the exercise, it would be worth asking pupils what words relating to food they already know (see Book 1, unit 3). This could be broken down into separate areas such as meat, vegetables and fruit. In this way, as a group, they would be in a position to recognise many of the words that follow in the conversation. Even if they do not recognise a word, they should be encouraged to write down any unknown words as they think they are spelt. These words could be clarified afterwards.

CD 1, track 12

Transcript:

Elena:	Hola, Jorge, ¿qué tal?
Jorge:	Muy bien, ¿y tú?
Elena:	Muy bien. ¿Adónde vas?
Jorge:	A Hipercor.
Elena:	¿Qué vas a comprar?
Jorge:	Comida, mucha comida.
Elena:	¡Cómo no! ¿Qué comida?
Jorge:	Primero, carne. Mucha carne.
Elena:	¿Qué carne?
Jorge:	Bueno, cuatro filetes de ternera, ocho pechugas de pollo, diez filetes de solomillo, treinta albóndigas, una pierna de cordero y, claro, un montón de hamburguesas.
Elena:	¡Madre mía!¿ Es que va el ejército a tu casa?
Jorge:	Más o menos. Vienen mis primos de Santander.
Elena:	¿Todos?
Jorge:	Sí, todos.
Elena:	Ya, entiendo. ¿Solamente vas a comprar carne?
Jorge:	No, hace falta comprar más cosas. El primer día vamos a hacer una paella. Entonces tengo que comprar arroz, cebollas, pimientos, ajo, y marisco.
Elena:	¿Qué tipo de marisco?
Jorge:	No sé. Gambas, mejillones, calamares.
Elena:	Y almejas. Hay que comprar almejas.
Jorge:	Sí, es verdad. También tengo que comprar muchas verduras y hortalizas.
Elena:	¿Por qué?
Jorge:	Porque las gemelas Carmen y Elvira son vegetarianas.
Elena:	Ya. ¿Qué vas a comprar?
Jorge:	Bueno, patatas, tomates, zanahorias, champiñones, judías verdes. Y cosas para hacer una ensalada. ¿Qué me sugieres?
Elena:	¿Qué tal, lechuga, pepino, aguacate? Ya has dicho tomates.
Jorge:	Y a mis primos les gustan mucho los postres. ¿Qué puedo comprar?
Elena:	Helado, flan, tarta, y, claro, fruta, mucha fruta.
Jorge:	¡Qué horror! La fruta no me gusta.
Elena:	A ti, no, pero a ellos, sí. Compra naranjas, manzanas, plátanos, peras.
Jorge:	Vale, vale.

Translation:

Elena:	Hi, Jorge, how are you?
Jorge:	Really well, and you?
Elena:	Really well. Where are you going?
Jorge:	To *Hipercor*.
Elena:	What are you going to buy?
Jorge:	Food, loads of food.
Elena:	Naturally. What type of food?
Jorge:	First of all, meat, lots of meat.
Elena:	What meat?
Jorge:	Well, four fillets of veal, eight chicken breasts, ten sirloin steaks, thirty meatballs, one leg of lamb, and, of course, loads of hamburgers.
Elena:	Good God! Are the Army coming round?
Jorge:	More or less. My cousins from Santander are coming.
Elena:	All of them?
Jorge:	Yes, all of them.
Elena:	Right, I understand now. Are you only going to buy meat?
Jorge:	No, I've got to buy other things too. On the first day we're going to do a paella. So, I've got to buy rice, onions, peppers, garlic and shellfish.
Elena:	What type of shellfish?
Jorge:	I'm not sure. Prawns, mussels, squid.
Elena:	And clams. You have to buy clams.
Jorge:	Oh, that's true. I've also got to buy loads of vegetables.
Elena:	Why?
Jorge:	Because the twins Carmen and Laura are vegetarian.
Elena:	Right. What vegetables are you going to buy?
Jorge:	Well, potatoes, tomatoes, carrots, mushrooms, green beans. And ingredients for a salad. Any suggestions?
Elena:	Well, how about lettuce, cucumber, avocado? You've already mentioned tomatoes.
Jorge:	And my cousins really like desserts. What can I buy?
Elena:	Ice-cream, crème caramel, cakes, and fruit, of course, lots of fruit.
Jorge:	How awful! I don't like fruit.
Elena:	You might not, but they do. Buy oranges, apples, bananas, pears.
Jorge:	OK, OK.

Answers to exercise:

La carne:
La ternera
Las pechugas de pollo
Los filetes de solomillo
Las albóndigas
La pierna de cordero
Las hamburguesas

La paella:
El arroz
Las cebollas
Los pimientos
El ajo
Las gambas
Los mejillones
Los calamares
Las almejas

Las verduras y hortalizas:
Las patatas
Los tomates
Las zanahorias
Los champiñones
Las judías verdes

La ensalada:
La lechuga
El pepino
El aguacate
Los tomates

El postre:
El helado
El flan
La tarta
Las naranjas
Las manzanas
Los plátanos
Las peras

Suggestions: After verifying that pupils understand all the food words in the conversation, individual pupils could be asked about what food **they** prefer, e.g. *¿Qué tipo de carne prefieres? ¿Qué tipo de fruta te gusta más? ¿Qué verduras te gustan?* The dialogue also involves several examples of the compound future (*ir + a + infinitive*). Further questions could be posed incorporating this use of the future, e.g. *¿Qué vas a comer esta noche/fin de semana?*

Exercise 2.2

A recording of the conversation is available on the CD.

CD 1, track 13

Angela:	*Bueno, Elena, ¿te apetece desayunar?*
Elena:	*¿Qué hora es?*
Angela:	*Son las ocho.*
Elena:	*Es un poco temprano, ¿no? En España no desayuno hasta las nueve.*
Angela:	*¿Y qué desayunas?*
Elena:	*Zumo de naranja, un café con leche y una tostada con aceite y tomate. ¡Qué rico!*
Angela:	*¡Qué asco! ¿Tostada con aceite? ¡Qué horror!*
Elena:	*¡Qué va! Está buenísimo. ¿Por qué no lo pruebas?*
Angela:	*No, gracias. ¿Y a qué hora almuerzas?*
Elena:	*Nunca comemos antes de las tres.*
Angela:	*¿Por qué?*
Elena:	*Porque mis padres no vuelven del trabajo hasta esa hora.*
Angela:	*¿Eso es normal?*
Elena:	*Sí. Muchas veces la gente deja de trabajar a eso de las dos y luego van a un bar a tomarse una cerveza antes de ir a casa para comer.*
Angela:	*¿Y qué sueles almorzar?*
Elena:	*Depende. De primer plato, sopa. Luego, normalmente, comemos carne con patatas fritas – pollo, solomillo, algo así. Y siempre tomamos ensalada. Y pan. El pan es muy importante.*

Angela:	¿Y de postre?
Elena:	Bueno, yo prefiero flan, pero mi madre me dice que coma fruta porque está muy bien para la salud.
Angela:	¿Y qué te gusta beber?
Elena:	A mí, me gustaría cerveza, pero cuando como con mis padres tomo agua con gas; no les gusta que beba alcohol.

Translation:

Angela:	Well, Elena, do you feel like breakfast?
Elena:	What time is it?
Angela:	Eight o'clock.
Elena:	It's a little early isn't it? In Spain I don't have breakfast until nine.
Angela:	And what do you have?
Elena:	Orange juice, white coffee, toast with olive oil and tomato. Absolutely delicious!
Angela:	How disgusting! Toast with oil? How awful!
Elena:	Quite the opposite. It's fantastic. Why don't you try it?
Angela:	No thank you. And when do you have lunch?
Elena:	We never eat before three.
Angela:	Why?
Elena:	Because my parents don't return from work until that time.
Angela:	Is that normal?
Elena:	Yes. Often people finish work around two and then they go and have a beer before going home for lunch.
Angela:	And what do you usually eat?
Elena:	It depends. Soup to start with. Then we normally have some type of meat with chips – chicken, sirloin, something like that. And we always have salad. And bread. Bread is really important.
Angela:	And dessert?
Elena:	Well, I prefer crème caramel, but my mum tells me to eat fruit as it's very healthy.
Angela:	And what do you have to drink?
Elena:	I would like beer, but when I eat with my parents I have fizzy water as they don't like me drinking alcohol.

Answers to questions:
1. *Porque en España se desayuna más tarde.*
2. *No le gusta nada.*
3. *Porque sus padres no vuelven hasta esa hora.*
4. *Van a tomarse una cerveza en un bar.*
5. *Fruta, puesto que es muy buena para la salud.*
6. *Cerveza, pero a sus padres no les gusta que beba alcohol.*

Translations:
1. Because breakfast is taken later in Spain.
2. She doesn't like it at all.
3. Because her parents don't get back until that time.
4. They go and have a beer in a bar.
5. Fruit, as it's really good for one's health.
6. Beer, but her parents don't like her drinking alcohol.

Suggestions: Clearly, it is necessary to clarify the answers to the questions orally. In addition, there are further questions that can be asked, e.g. *¿A Elena, qué le gusta desayunar? ¿Qué suele comer para el almuerzo?* This could then lead to more personal questions directed at individual pupils asking them to state their own preferences and likes and dislikes. They could be encouraged to use words or phrases such as *suelo desayunar………., me gusta……………, normalmente comemos a las……….*

Exercise 2.3

Suggestions: Pupils should be encouraged to come to the front of the class in their pairs and to enact their dialogues. You could add an extra dimension here: you could list a number of adjectives on the board/OHP such as *enfadado, loco, triste, contentísimo* and tell the pupils reading the dialogue to choose one, but to keep it to themselves. They would then enact their part of the dialogue in keeping with the adjective. Clarification should be made with the rest of the class at the end of the dialogue. As usual, questions should be posed to the class about the content of each dialogue, e.g. *¿Cuándo desayuna? ¿Qué suele comer y beber para el desayuno?* Pupils should always be encouraged to answer in full sentences. As ever, it is worthwhile getting them to take notes, as memories are often fallible.

Exercise 2.4

Suggestions: Before beginning the exercise, pupils could be asked to name some food words that they already know that are similar in Spanish and in English.

Answers to exercise:

1.	Atún, el	=	tuna
2.	Coco, el	=	coconut
3.	Coliflor, la	=	cauliflower
4.	Ensalada, la	=	salad
5.	Espaguetis, los	=	spaghetti
6.	Espinacas, las	=	spinach
7.	Fruta, la	=	fruit
8.	Hamburguesa, la	=	hamburger
9.	Jamón, el	=	ham
10.	Lasaña, la	=	lasagne
11.	Limón, el	=	lemon
12.	Mandarina, la	=	mandarin
13.	Melón, el	=	melon
14.	Pasta, la	=	pasta
15.	Patata, la	=	potato
16.	Pera, la	=	pear
17.	Piña, la	=	pineapple
18.	Pizza, la	=	pizza
19.	Salmón, el	=	salmon
20.	Sopa, la	=	soup
21.	Tomate, el	=	tomato

Exercise 2.5

Answers to exercise:

	ALMORZAR	PREFERIR	QUERER	SOLER
Yo	almuerzo	prefiero	quiero	suelo
Tú	almuerzas	prefieres	quieres	sueles
Él	almuerza	prefiere	quiere	suele
Nosotros	almorzamos	preferimos	queremos	solemos
Vosotros	almorzáis	preferís	queréis	soléis
Ellos	almuerzan	prefieren	quieren	suelen

Exercise 2.6

This exercise provides valuable practice at the use of the verbs revised in Exercise 2.6.

Exercise 2.7

Suggested answers to exercise (in bold):

Pepe es un dormilón. Entonces no **desayuna** hasta las once. Le **gusta** tomar una tostada y un **café** con leche. También, normalmente **bebe/toma** un zumo de naranja. No **almuerza** hasta las tres, porque sus padres trabajan y no **vuelven/regresan** a casa hasta esa hora. Le **gustaría** beber vino, pero sus padres no le dejan. Por la noche **cena** a las diez. Le gusta **mucho/comer** la carne y, de **postre,** helado de vainilla.

Translation:
Pepe is a real sleepy head. Therefore, he doesn't have breakfast until eleven. He likes to have toast and white coffee. Normally, he also has an orange juice. He doesn't have lunch until three because his parents work and don't return home until that time. He would like to drink wine, but his parents don't let him. At night he has dinner at ten. He really likes meat and vanilla ice-cream for dessert.

Exercise 2.8
CD 1, track 14

Transcript:

Camarera:	¿Puedo tomar nota?
Jorge:	Yo creo que sí. ¿Has decidido, cariño?
Elena:	Sí, cariño.
Jorge:	¿Qué te apetece?
Elena:	De primero la sopa de pescado.
Camarera:	Muy bien, señora.
Elena (con enfado)**:**	Señorita, por favor.
Camarera:	Lo siento. ¿De segundo plato, señorita?
Elena:	La ensalada de espinacas y zanahorias. ¿Estará buena, no?
Camarera:	Buenísima, señorita. ¿Y Usted, señor?
Jorge:	De primero, la sopa de cebolla. Y luego…………..¿No tienen hamburguesas?
Camarera:	Lo siento señor. Éste es un restaurante de lujo. No tenemos hamburguesas.
Jorge:	¿No tienen hamburguesas? ¡Qué barbaridad! Entonces, ¿qué carne hay? Me apetece carne.
Camarera:	Tenemos albóndigas, chuletas, jamón asado, cordero, pollo, solomillo.
Jorge:	¿Pero hamburguesas no?
Camarera:	No, señor, hamburguesas no.
Jorge:	Entonces, póngame dos solomillos de cerdo.

Camarera:	¿Dos, señor?
Jorge:	Sí. ¿Pasa algo?
Camarera:	No, señor. ¿Cómo los quiere, señor?
Jorge:	Pues en un plato. ¿Cómo los voy a querer?
Camarera:	¿Poco hecho, medio....?
Jorge:	Ah, ya, ya. Poco hecho. Y con patatas fritas.
Camarera:	Cómo no, señor.

Translation:

Camarera:	Can I take your order?
Jorge:	I think so. Have you decided darling?
Elena:	Yes, darling.
Jorge:	What do you feel like?
Elena:	Fish soup to start with.
Camarera:	Fine señora.
Elena (angrily)**:**	It's señorita.
Camarera:	Sorry. And as your main?
Elena:	The spinach and carrot salad. It will be good, won't it?
Camarera:	Fantastic, señorita. And you sir?
Jorge:	I'll have the onion soup to start with. And then……….Don't you have hamburguers?
Camarera:	I'm sorry sir. This is a cordon bleu restaurant. We don't have hamburguers.
Jorge:	You don't have hamburguers? How extraordinary! What meat do you have then? I feel like meat.
Camarera:	We've got meatballs, chops, roasted ham, lamb, chicken, sirloin.
Jorge:	But no hamburguers?
Camarera:	No sir, no hamburguers.
Jorge:	Well then, I'll have two sirloin fillets.
Camarera:	Two sir?
Jorge:	Yes. Is there a problem?
Camarera:	No sir. How would you like them?
Jorge:	On a plate naturally. How else would I want them?
Camarera:	Rare, medium….
Jorge:	Ah, I see. Rare. And with chips.
Camarera:	No problem, sir.

Suggestions: The following questions should be asked:
1. *¿Qué piden Elena y Jorge de primer plato?*
2. *¿Qué piden de segundo plato?*
3. *¿Por qué Jorge no puede comer hamburguesas?*
4. *¿Cómo quiere la carne Jorge?*

Answers:
1. *Elena pide sopa de pescado, y Jorge pide sopa de cebolla.*
2. *Elena pide ensalada de espinacas y zanahorias, y Jorge pide dos solomillos de cerdo con patatas fritas.*
3. *Porque es un restaurante de lujo y no hay hamburguesas.*
4. *La quiere poco hecha.*

Homework: Either individually, or in groups of three, pupils could be asked to provide their own conclusion to this dialogue. This could then be enacted, if appropriate, in class. Also, a vocabulary test could be set on all the words in the original dialogue.

Exercise 2.9

A recording of the passage is available on the CD.

CD 1, track 15

Camarera:	¿Le ha gustado la ensalada, señorita?
Elena:	Mucho. Estaba buenísima.
Camarera:	¿Qué tal el solomillo, señor? ¿Estaba rico?
Jorge:	Sí, muy sabroso, pero los filetes eran un poco pequeños para mí.
Camarera:	Lo siento. ¿Les apetece algo de postre?
Elena:	Yo no puedo, gracias. Estoy llenísima.
Camarera:	¿De verdad? Tenemos tarta de queso, tarta de manzana, arroz con leche, mousse de chocolate.
Elena:	Es que no puedo.
Jorge:	Yo sí. ¿Tienen helado, o los restaurantes de lujo tampoco tienen helado?
Camarera:	Sí, señor, tenemos helado.
Jorge:	¿De qué sabores?
Camarera:	De fresa, vainilla, chocolate, de plátano con chocolate....
Jorge:	Póngame uno de fresa y vainilla, por favor. El chocolate me gusta, pero me da dolor de cabeza.
Camarera:	Muy bien. ¿Ya está?
Jorge:	No. Me apetece también arroz con leche. ¿Me lo trae después del helado, por favor?
Camarera:	¿Arroz con leche también?
Jorge:	Sí. ¿Hay algún problema?
Camarera:	Conmigo, no.
Jorge:	¿Quiere decir que yo sí tengo algún problema?
Camarera:	Claro que no señor.¿ Les pongo algo más de beber?
Jorge:	Sí, otra cerveza para mí. ¿Y tú, Elena?
Elena:	Yo quiero otra botella de agua con gas.
Camarera:	Ahora mismo.

Translation:

Camarera:	Did you like the salad, señorita?
Elena:	Very much. It was delicious.
Camarera:	How was the sirloin, sir? Was it good?
Jorge:	Yes, very tasty, but the fillets were a little small for me.
Camarera:	I'm sorry. Would you like anything for dessert?
Elena:	I couldn't, thank you. I'm full.
Camarera:	Really? We've got cheesecake, apple pie, rice pudding, chocolate mousse
Elena:	I just couldn't.
Jorge:	I could. Do you have any ice-cream or don't high-class restaurants do ice-cream either?
Camarera:	Yes, sir, we do have ice-cream.
Jorge:	What flavours?
Camarera:	Strawberry, vanilla, chocolate, banana with chocolate.
Jorge:	I'll have strawberry and vanilla. I like chocolate, but it gives me headaches.
Camarera:	Very good. Is that all?
Jorge:	No, I'll have some rice pudding. Could you bring it to me after the ice-cream please?
Camarera:	Rice pudding too?
Jorge:	Yes. Is there a problem?
Camarera:	Not with me.
Jorge:	Do you mean to say that I have a problem?

Camarera:	No, of course not sir. Would you like anything else to drink?
Jorge:	Yes, another beer for me. And you, Elena?
Elena:	I'd like another fizzy water.
Camarera:	Right away.

Answers to questions:
1. *Buenísima, rico, sabroso.*
2. *Está llenísima; no puede comer más.*
3. *Tienen de fresa, vainilla, chocolate, plátano con chocolate.*
4. *Le da dolor de cabeza.*
5. *Jorge pide una cerveza y Elena pide agua con gas.*

Translations:
1. The 3 words for tasty are: *buenísima, rico, sabroso.*
2. She's full; she can't eat any more.
3. They have vanilla, chocolate, banana with chocolate.
4. It gives him a headache.
5. Jorge orders a beer and Elena fizzy water.

Suggestions: Depending on pupils' standard, they could be encouraged to try to answer, where possible, using their own words. For example for question 2, they could answer *porque no puede comer más*, rather than copying directly from the text. Again, there is much scope for oral work here. Once the answers have been gone through, pupils could be asked questions about their own preferences as far as desserts and drink are concerned. They could be encouraged to use hugely important words such as *apetecer*, e.g. *normalmente, ¿qué te apetece de postre?* If they appear to be struggling, you could prompt them by stating preferences of your own, e.g. *a mí muchas veces me apetece queso, otras veces me apetece helado.* This could lead on to reinforcement of the flavours, e.g. *¿qué sabores de helado te gustán más/menos?*

Exercise 2.10

Suggestions: Before starting the exercise, it is important to establish that pupils have all the necessary vocabulary. They should be familiar with words such as *pedir, apetecer, bocadillo* etc, but one can never be too careful! After the exercise has been completed it should be written up on the board/OHP using ideas from the pupils themselves. Grammar points could be elaborated when going through the translation. For example, one should mention that because *hambre* is a noun rather than an adjective, it takes *mucha* and not *muy*. Furthermore, one could stress the importance of differentiating between *preguntar* (to ask you a question) and *pedir* (to ask for something).

Translation:
The translation is available on CD 1, track 16.

CD 1, track 16

Carlos:	Tengo mucha hambre. Quiero pedir.
Manolo:	Yo también. ¿Qué te apetece?
Carlos:	Me apetece un bocadillo de jamón. ¿Y a ti?
Manolo:	Para mí, una hamburguesa con muchas patatas fritas.
Carlos:	¿Qué te gustaría beber?
Manolo:	Yo voy a tomar una cerveza. ¿Y tú?
Carlos:	Me gustaría una cerveza, pero si entra Mamá…..
Manolo:	Mejor pedir otra cosa.
Carlos:	Sí, creo que tienes razón.

Exercise 2.11
Suggestions: Pupils should be encouraged to enact their dialogues. The others should be posed questions afterwards. This is a good exercise in terms of getting them to think about how the different parts of a verb work. Their tendency will be to repeat exactly what they have heard (in the first person), when, in fact, they will need to change the verb to the third person, e.g. **quiere** comer un bocadillo de queso rather than **quiero**.

Soler
Yo suelo   Nosotros solemos
Tú sueles   Vosotros soléis
Él suele   Ellos suelen

Exercise 2.12
Answers to exercise:
1. Suelo almorzar a la una.
2. Solemos pedir cerveza.
3. Suelen tener mucha hambre a las cuatro.
4. ¿Sueles comer/tomar postre?
5. Suele cenar con su hermano.

Translations:
1. I usually have lunch at one.
2. We usually order beer.
3. They're usually very hungry at four o'clock.
4. Do you usually have dessert?
5. He usually has dinner with his brother.

Translation of questions 6-8:
6. ¿Sueles comer naranjas?
7. ¿Sueles comer jamón?
8. ¿Sueles comer bocadillos?

Answers to questions:
6. No/Sí, las suelo comer; or suelo comerlas.
7. No/Sí, lo suelo comer; or suelo comerlo.
8. No/Sí, los suelo comer; or suelo comerlos.

Exercise 2.13
Answers to exercise (in bold):
Carlos **suele** levantarse a las ocho. Baja con su hermano para tomar el desayuno. Los dos **lo** comen juntos. A Manolo le gusta el café, pero siempre **lo** toma con azúcar. Carlos prefiere leche. **La** toma muy, muy fría. Los hermanos van al mismo instituto y **suelen** almorzar juntos. Por la noche **suelen** tomar la cena con sus padres. **La** toman a eso de las nueve. Carlos **suele** acostarse a las once, y su hermano **suele** acostarse un poco más tarde.

Translation:
Carlos usually gets up at eight o'clock. He goes downstairs with his brother to eat breakfast. The two usually eat together. *Manolo* likes coffee, but he always has it with sugar. *Carlos* prefers milk. He takes it very, very cold. The brothers go to the same school and usually have lunch together. In the evening they usually have dinner with their parents. They eat it around nine o'clock. *Carlos* usually goes to bed at eleven and his brother usually goes to bed a little bit later.

Exercise 2.14

Answers to exercise (in bold):
Yo **suelo levantarme** a las ocho. **Bajo** con **mi** hermano para tomar el desayuno. Los dos lo **comemos** juntos. A Manolo le gusta el café, pero siempre lo toma con azúcar. **Yo prefiero** leche. La **tomo** muy, muy fría. **Vamos** al mismo instituto y **solemos** almorzar juntos. Por la noche **solemos** tomar la cena con **nuestros** padres. La **tomamos** a eso de las nueve. **Yo suelo acostarme** a las once, y **mi** hermano **suele** acostarse un poco más tarde.

After going through the exercise, pupils could be asked what their and their families' habits are, e.g. ¿Cuándo soléis almorzar los domingos? or ¿Qué sueles desayunar los sábados?

Revision
Now would be a good time to see just how many new words relating to food and drink pupils have absorbed. They could be asked to list all the words they can remember under the following categories: *carne, fruta, postre, bebidas, otro.* They could then be asked to read out individual examples which others could be asked to translate. This might also be a good time to introduce the 'market game'. The class should be divided into groups of five or six. Group 1 starts with a pupil who says *Voy al mercado para comer manzanas.* A member of group 2 then says *Voy al mercado para comer manzanas y naranjas* and so on around the class. If a group gets the sequence wrong or forgets an item, they are eliminated.

Exercise 2.15

N.B. You will see that there is no vocabulary list for this exercise in the pupils' book. Pupils should be encouraged to answer the questions as best they can without being given any words. Any unknown words can be clarified afterwards.

CD 1, track 17

Transcript:

Poppy:	¿Adónde vamos a comer esta noche?
Carmen:	A un restaurante chino.
Poppy:	¿Un restaurante chino?
Carmen:	Sí, hay muchos en España.
Poppy:	¿Y qué otros tipos de restaurantes hay?
Carmen:	Bueno, los hay de comida italiana, alemana….
Poppy:	¿Alemana?
Carmen:	Sí, como a la gente le gusta tanto la carne y la cerveza.
Poppy:	¿Y hay muchos restaurantes vegetarianos?
Carmen:	No lo sé. Creo que no. Aquí se come mucha carne. ¿Te parece bien la comida china?
Poppy:	Sí, claro. A mí, me gusta todo menos la fruta.
Carmen:	¿De verdad? Entonces tengo que presentarte a mi amigo Jorge. A él tampoco le gusta la fruta. Por curiosidad, ¿te gustan las hamburguesas?
Poppy:	Me encantan. ¿A tu amigo Jorge, también?
Carmen:	Pues sí. ¿Qué tipo de comida se come en Inglaterra?
Poppy:	Hay de todo. Comida francesa, italiana, china, india, mejicana. También, hay muchísimos restaurantes españoles. A mí me encanta la comida española, sobre todo la paella. ¡Qué maravilla! Es que el arroz me gusta mucho.
Carmen:	Yo prefiero la comida italiana. La pasta para mí es una delicia.
Poppy:	¿Y qué te gusta beber? Yo prefiero los refrescos. No soporto el alcohol.
Carmen:	Aquí se bebe mucha cerveza, vino, y, claro, las copas.
Poppy:	¿Qué son las copas?
Carmen:	Son bebidas como el whisky, el vodka, el ron, mezcladas con, por ejemplo, coca-cola, o fanta, o tónica.
Poppy:	¡Qué asco!

Translation:

Poppy:	Where are we going to eat this evening?
Carmen:	A Chinese restaurant.
Poppy:	A Chinese restaurant?
Carmen:	Yes, there are lots in Spain.
Poppy:	And what other types of food are there?
Carmen:	Well, Italian, German.
Poppy:	German?
Carmen:	Yes, as people are so fond of meat and beer.
Poppy:	And are there a lot of vegetarian restaurants?
Carmen:	I don't know. I don't think so. We eat a lot of meat here. Are you ok with Chinese?
Poppy:	Yes, of course. I like everything except fruit.
Carmen:	Really? Then I must introduce you to my friend Jorge. He doesn't like fruit either. Out of curiosity, do you like hamburgers?
Poppy:	I love them. Does your friend Jorge like them too?
Carmen:	Well, yes. What type of food do you eat in England?
Poppy:	There's everything: French, Italian, Chinese, Indian, Mexican. Also, there are loads of Spanish restaurants. I love Spanish food, especially paella. How fantastic! The thing is I love rice.
Carmen:	I prefer Italian. For me, pasta is absolutely delicious.
Poppy:	And what do you like to drink. I prefer soft drinks. I can't stand alcohol.
Carmen:	People drink a lot of beer and wine here and of course *copas*.
Poppy:	What are *copas*?
Carmen:	They're drinks like whisky, vodka, rum, mixed with things like coca-cola, fanta, or tonic water.
Poppy:	How disgusting!

Answers to questions:
1. *Hay comida china, italiana, alemana.*
2. *Porque a la gente le gusta mucho la carne.*
3. *Le gusta todo menos la fruta.*
4. *No les gusta la fruta y les encantan las hamburguesas.*
5. *La comida francesa, la italiana, la china, la india, la mejicana, la española.*
6. *Prefiere la comida italiana.*
7. *Le gustan los refrescos.*
8. *Son bebidas como el whisky o el ron mezcladas con un refresco como fanta o coca-cola.*

Homework: Pupils could be asked to do a survey about the different cuisines people prefer as well as eating times. Results could be established and compared in class in Spanish. Findings could be expressed thus: *En mi encuesta, la gente prefiere la comida francesa, después la italiana, y después la española.* This could then lead on to revision of numbers. For example, individual pupils could be asked *¿En tu encuesta, cuántas personas prefieren la comida italiana?* Perhaps there is scope for information to be entered into a database.

Exercise 2.16

Una cena romántica – segunda parte
A recording is available on the CD.

CD 1, track 18

Transcript:

Jorge: *Oye, Manolo, necesito tu ayuda. Como sabes, muy pronto va a ser el día de San Valentín, y Elena está muy enfadada conmigo.*

Manolo:	¿Por qué?
Jorge:	Por lo del otro día en el restaurante.
Manolo:	Ah, sí. ¿Qué tal?
Jorge:	Fatal.
Manolo:	¿Por qué?
Jorge:	Por la camarera. ¡Qué mujer más antipática! Quiero arreglarlo. Quiero prepararle a Elena una comida buenísima. ¿Quieres ayudarme?
Manolo:	Claro. ¿Qué tipo de comida le gusta?
Jorge:	Le gusta todo: la comida italiana, la china, la francesa, incluso la comida inglesa.
Manolo:	¿La comida inglesa? ¿Está loca?
Jorge:	Un poco. El problema es que dice que está muy gorda y por eso siempre pide ensaladas.
Manolo:	¡Qué lástima!
Jorge:	¡De verdad!
Manolo:	Pero bueno, se puede hacer una ensalada muy rica.
Jorge:	¿Con qué?
Manolo:	Con los ingredientes normales. Para empezar: lechuga, tomate, cebolla, ajo, con aceite de oliva. Luego se le pueden echar otras cosas. ¿Le gustan la fruta y la carne?
Jorge:	Sí, mucho.
Manolo:	Entonces, vamos a echarle piña, kiwi, plátano y pollo.
Jorge:	¿Piña, kiwi, plátano y pollo?
Manolo:	Sí, le va a encantar.
Jorge:	Espero que sí.

Translation:

Jorge:	Listen, Manolo, I need your help. As you know, it's Saint Valentine's Day very soon and Elena is really angry with me.
Manolo:	Why?
Jorge:	Because of what happened in the restaurant the other day.
Manolo:	Oh, yes. How was it?
Jorge:	Terrible.
Manolo:	Why?
Jorge:	Because of the waitress. What an unpleasant woman. I want to fix things. I want to make her a really nice meal. Do you want to help me?
Manolo:	Of course. What type of food does she like?
Jorge:	Everything: Italian, Chinese, French, even English food.
Manolo:	English food? Is she mad?
Jorge:	A little bit. The problem is she always says she's very fat and so she always orders salads.
Manolo:	What a pity!
Jorge:	Absolutely!
Manolo:	But, even so, one can still make a delicious salad.
Jorge:	What with?
Manolo:	The normal ingredients to begin with: lettuce, tomato, onion, garlic, olive oil. Then you can add other things. Does she like fruit and meat?
Jorge:	Yes, very much.
Manolo:	In that case, let's add some pineapple, kiwi, banana and chicken.
Jorge:	Pineapple, kiwi, banana and chicken?
Manolo:	Yes, she'll love it.
Jorge:	I hope so.

Answers to questions:
1. Quiere prepararle una comida buenísima a Elena.
2. Dice que era muy antipática.
3. Porque le gusta la comida inglesa.
4. Porque dice que está gorda.
5. Además de los ingredientes normales, la ensalada de Manolo tiene fruta (piña, kiwi, plátano) y carne (pollo).

Exercise 2.17

Answers to exercise:
1. Esta paella está buenísima/fantástica/estupenda/riquísima.
2. Ella es de España.
3. La comida está en la mesa.
4. Estas naranjas están deliciosas.
5. Jorge está contento porque la carne está buena.

Suggestions: It would be worth establishing the different ways one could translate delicious, as in sentence 1. It would also be worth stressing the importance of the accent in *está*. Otherwise, of course, the word turns into the demonstrative adjective *esta* as at the beginning of sentence 1.

To reinforce the different criteria for *ser* and *estar*, pupils could be asked to invent some sentences of their own using examples of both verbs. They should also be encouraged to use different parts of each verb.

Exercise 2.18

Translation of recipe:
Ingredients:
1 lettuce
100 g of rice
2 bananas
50 g of prunes
Water
A few drops of lemon juice
Salt

For the dressing:
Vinegar
1 teaspoonful of mustard
Brown sugar
Salt
Oregano
Olive oil

Preparation:
Cook the rice in water with a few drops of lemon juice and salt, run it under cold water and drain well. Wash the lettuce and cut it up thinly, and then put it in a salad bowl along with the bananas which should have been skinned and sliced up. Add the rice and mix all the ingredients well. Add the prunes. In a separate container, mix the teaspoonful of mustard with a little vinegar, salt and a touch of sugar. Add the olive oil and the oregano, mix well and add this as dressing to the salad.

UNIT 2 | 33

Answers to questions:
1. El arroz se cuece primero con zumo de limón y sal, y luego se pasa por agua y se escurre bien.
2. La lechuga se lava, se corta y se coloca en una ensaladera.
3. Se agrega el arroz y se mezclan bien los ingredientes. Luego, se añaden las pasas.
4. En el recipiente aparte se prepara el aliño.

Translations:
1. The rice is cooked first with lemon juice and salt, and is then run under cold water and drained well.
2. The lettuce is washed, cut and placed in a salad bowl.
3. The rice is added and the ingredients mixed well. Then the prunes are added.
4. It is used for preparing the dressing.

Suggestions: The pupils may have chosen alternative ways to answer the questions, but, regardless, it would be sensible to point out the usefulness of using the word *se* in situations such as these.

Exercise 2.19
CD 1, track 19

Transcript:

Lucía:	¡Diga!
Carmen:	Hola Lucía, soy Carmen. Necesito tu ayuda. Tengo que hacer una paella para mi amiga inglesa, y no sé cómo hacerla. ¿Cuáles son los ingredientes?
Lucía:	Bueno, hay muchas paellas diferentes, pero ésta es una receta de Arguiñano y siempre está muy rica. Necesitas 200g. de rape, 200g. de gambas, 200g. de almejas, 8 langostinos y sal.
Carmen:	¿Ya está?
Lucía:	¡Qué va! También necesitas perejil, 400g. de arroz, 1 cebolla picada, 1 zanahoria picada, 1 pimiento verde picado y 2 dientes de ajo picados.
Carmen:	¿Y qué tengo que hacer con todo eso?
Lucía:	Coge una paellera y rehoga la verdura cinco minutos. Luego, añade el pescado, las gambas y las almejas. Rehoga bien e incorpora el arroz. Echa un poco de sal, y cuando empiece a hervir, coloca los langostinos encima y deja cocer quince minutos a fuego suave.
Carmen:	¡Madre mía! ¿Y cómo se llama esta paella?
Lucía:	Paella Sencilla.
Carmen:	¡Sí, muy sencilla!

Translation:

Lucía:	Hello.
Carmen:	Hello, Lucía, it's Carmen. I need your help. I have to make a paella for my English friend, and I don't know how to do it. What are the ingredients?
Lucía:	Well there are lots of different types of paella, but this is a recipe of *Arguiñano* and it's always really tasty. You need 200 g of anglerfish, 200 g of prawns, 200 g of clams, 8 king prawns and salt.
Carmen:	Is that it?
Lucía:	No way! You also need parsley, 400 g of rice, 1 sliced onion, 1 sliced carrot, 1 sliced green pepper, and 2 sliced cloves of garlic.
Carmen:	And what do I have to do with all that lot?
Lucía:	Get a pan for the paella and sauté the vegetables for five minutes. Then, add the fish, the prawns, and the clams. Sauté well and add the rice. Add a bit of salt, and when it starts to boil, put the king prawns on top and let it all simmer for fifteen minutes.
Carmen:	Good Lord! What's this paella called?
Lucía:	Simple Paella.
Carmen:	Yes, right. Really simple!

Suggestions: Clearly, there may be some words such as *rape* that the pupils have not come across before, but they should be asked to write down as many words as they can, and any unknown words can be clarified afterwards. The excerpt should be played as many times as deemed necessary.

Answers:
Ingredientes:
200g. de rape
200g. de gambas
200g. de almejas
8 langostinos
Sal
Perejil
400g. de arroz
1 cebolla
1 zanahoria
1 pimiento
2 dientes de ajo

Elaboración:
Coge una paellera y rehoga la verdura cinco minutos. Luego, añade el pescado, las gambas y las almejas. Rehoga bien e incorpora el arroz. Echa un poco de sal, y cuando empiece a hervir, coloca los langostinos encima y deja cocer quince minutos a fuego suave.

Exercise 2.20

Suggestions: Pupils should be encouraged to read out their recipes. The rest of the class should be instructed to take notes with a view to trying to answer teacher-led questions afterwards.

Homework: Pupils should, by now, have a wide vocabulary as far as this topic is concerned. However, as homework, they could be told to find a defined number of additional words. On one day this could be words relating to fruit, on another drink etc. Words could be shared in class and added to individual vocabulary lists.

Exercise 2.21
CD 1, track 20

Transcript:

Antonio:	*¡Oiga, por favor!*
Camarera:	*Buenas noches, señores. ¿Tomo nota ya?*
Antonio:	*Sí, por favor. María, ¿qué vas a tomar?*
María:	*De primero, me apetecen unos mejillones. Luego, de segundo, un solomillo bastante hecho. Me pone también una ensalada de tomate, aguacate y cebolla.*
Antonio:	*Veo que tienes mucha hambre. Ya que hace calor, y yo tengo tanta sed como hambre, voy a empezar con el gazpacho. Luego, de segundo plato, voy a tomar una ración de tortilla española. De beber, me apetece vino. ¿Te apetece un poco de vino, María?*
María:	*Sí, vale.*
Antonio:	*De segundo, vas a tomar carne. ¿Qué tal una botella de vino tinto de la casa?*
María:	*Vale.*
Camarera:	*Muy bien, señores.*

UNIT 2 | 35

Translation:
Antonio: Excuse me!
Camarera: Good evening Sir, Madam. Are you ready to order?
Antonio: Yes please. María, what are you going to have?
María: As a starter, I feel like some mussels. Then, for the main, the steak, reasonably well done. Could I also have the tomato, avocado and onion salad?
Antonio: I see you're really hungry. As it's hot and I'm both thirsty and hungry, I'll start with the *gazpacho*. Then, for the main, I'll have a portion of *Spanish omelette*. I feel like some wine. Do you feel like a bit of wine, María?
María: Yes, all right.
Antonio: You're having meat for your main. How about a bottle of house red?
María: Fine.
Camarera: Very well.

Suggestions: The purpose of this exercise is to try to get the pupils to string together several words and phrases. Therefore, rather than just answer with one or two words, they should be encouraged to piece together bits of information. For example, in response to *¿Qué va a tomar María?* rather than simply responding *mejillones*, they should be aiming at *De primero va a tomar mejillones, de segundo solomillo bastante hecho y una ensalada también*. This reply could then ellicit another question such as *¿Qué ingredientes tiene la ensalada?*

Questions:
1. *¿Qué va a tomar María?*
2. *¿Qué ingredientes quiere María en la ensalada?*
3. *¿Qué va a tomar Antonio?*
4. *¿Qué van a beber?*

Answers:
1. *De primero, va a tomar mejillones; de segundo, solomillo bastante hecho y una ensalada también.*
2. *Quiere tomate, aguacate y cebolla.*
3. *Quiere gazpacho, de primero, y, de segundo, una ración de tortilla española.*
4. *Van a beber una botella de vino tinto de la casa.*

Exercise 2.22
CD 1, track 20

Answer to exercise:
Camarero: *Buenos días. ¿Qué va a tomar?*
Cliente: *De primero, la sopa de pescado y de segundo, un filete de ternera.*
Camarero: *¿Cómo lo quiere?*
Cliente: *Poco hecho por favor.*
Camarero: *¿Quiere una ensalada o alguna guarnición con la carne?*
Cliente: *Unas patatas fritas.*
Camarero: *¿Y de beber?*
Cliente: *Media botella de vino tinto y un botellín de agua con gas.*
Camarero: *Muy bien, señor.*

Translation:
Waiter: Hello. What would you like?
Customer: The fish soup to start with and fillet of veal for the main.

Waiter:	How would you like that done?
Customer:	Rare please.
Waiter:	Would you like a salad or some garnish with the meat?
Customer:	Some chips.
Waiter:	And to drink?
Customer:	Half a bottle of red wine and a small bottle of fizzy water.
Waiter:	Very well, sir.

Exercise 2.23

The conversation is available, with the gaps filled, on the CD.

CD 1, track 22

Answers to exercise (in bold):

Pepe:	¿**Quieres** merendar?
Yolanda:	No, tengo **mucha** hambre. Voy a pedir algunas tapas.
Pepe:	¿**Qué** tapas quieres?
Yolanda:	Voy a **tomar** pollo al ajillo y ensaladilla rusa.
Pepe:	¿Qué **ingredientes** tiene la ensaladilla rusa?
Yolanda:	Creo que mayonesa, atún, gambas, patatas y aceitunas.
Pepe:	A mí también me **apetece**. También **quiero** boquerones en vinagre y huevos rellenos.
Yolanda:	¿Qué **tal** unos mejillones al vapor?
Pepe:	**Vale** ¿Qué quieres **beber**?
Yolanda:	Yo, un **zumo** de naranja. ¿Y **tú**?
Pepe:	Yo, **una** cerveza.
Yolanda:	Lo **siento**. No puedes.

Translation:

Pepe:	Do you feel like an afternoon snack?
Yolanda:	No, I'm really hungry. I'm going to order some *tapas*.
Pepe:	Which *tapas* would you like?
Yolanda:	I'm going to have garlic chicken and Russian salad.
Pepe:	What ingredients are there in Russian salad?
Yolanda:	I think there's mayonnaise, tuna, prawns, potatoes and olives.
Pepe:	I feel like some too. I also want some anchovies in vinegar and stuffed eggs.
Yolanda:	How about some steamed mussels?
Pepe:	Fine. What do you want to drink?
Yolanda:	I'll have an orange juice, and you?
Pepe:	I'll have a beer.
Yolanda:	I'm sorry. You can't.

Exercise 2.24

Suggestions: Before asking questions about the dialogue, it is obviously important that pupils have read and understood the introduction to Christmas in Spain which comes prior to this exercise. As such, words such as *mantecados* and *pavo* should be able to be identified. The dialogue is also a good example of precisely the type of situation when the *Usted* mode of address is required. Furthermore one should allude to the importance of the verb *poner* when it comes to ordering food. This, of course, could apply in a cafeteria or restaurant. There is scope here for more role-play work which could reinforce the use of both *Usted* and *poner*.

CD 1, track 23

Transcript:

Dependienta:	Dígame señora. ¿Qué le pongo?
Elvira:	Póngame un kilo de langostinos, por favor.
Dependienta:	¿Algo más?
Elvira:	¿Están buenas las gambas?
Dependienta:	Buenísimas, señora.
Elvira:	Entonces, póngame quinientos gramos de gambas.
Dependienta:	¿Algo más?
Elvira:	También me hacen falta carne, patatas y cosas para hacer una ensalada. ¿Dónde puedo comprar eso?
Dependienta:	Aquí mismo señora. ¿Qué más le pongo?
Elvira:	Necesito un pavo grande, tres kilos de patatas, una lechuga, cuatro tomates grandes, un pepino, medio kilo de cebollas, y tres aguacates.
Dependienta:	¿Algo más?
Elvira:	¿Cómo están las piñas?
Dependienta:	Muy ricas, señora.
Elvira:	Póngame una bastante grande.
Dependienta:	¿Desea algo más?
Elvira:	Necesito mantecados, turrón, cava y anís. ¿Dónde puedo encontrar todo eso?
Dependienta:	El cava y el anís están allí, a la derecha, donde todos los vinos. Y los mantecados y el turrón están al lado de los vinos.
Elvira:	Muchas gracias.
Dependienta:	De nada. ¡Feliz Navidad!
Elvira:	Igualmente.

Translation:

Dependienta:	How can I help you, Madam?
Elvira:	A kilo of king prawns please.
Dependienta:	Anything else?
Elvira:	Are the prawns tasty?
Dependienta:	Extremely, Madam.
Elvira:	Then, I'll have 500 grams.
Dependienta:	Anything else?
Elvira:	I also need meat, potatoes, and ingredients to make a salad. Where can I buy all that?
Dependienta:	Right here, Madam. What else can I get you?
Elvira:	I need a large turkey, 3 kilos of potatoes, a lettuce, 4 big tomatoes, a cucumber, half a kilo of onions and 3 avocados.
Dependienta:	Anything else?
Elvira:	What are the pineapples like?
Dependienta:	Delicious, Madam.
Elvira:	Could you find me a pretty big one?
Dependienta:	Would you like anything else?
Elvira:	I need *mantecados*, nougat, sparkling wine and anisette. Where can I buy all that?
Dependienta:	The sparkling wine and anisette are there, over on the right, where all the wine is. And the *mantecados* and nougat are next to the wine section.
Elvira:	Many thanks.
Dependienta:	You're welcome. Happy Christmas!
Elvira:	The same to you.

Questions:
1. ¿Qué pide Elvira primero?
2. ¿Cuántos gramos de gambas pide?
3. ¿Qué carne compra?
4. ¿Qué ingredientes compra para la ensalada?
5. ¿Qué fruta pide?
6. ¿Qué bebida pide?
7. ¿Dónde están el turrón y los mantecados?

Answers:
1. *Pide 1 kilo de langostinos.*
2. *500.*
3. *Un pavo grande.*
4. *1 lechuga, 4 tomates grandes, 1 pepino, medio kilo de cebollas y 3 aguacates.*
5. *Pide 1 piña.*
6. *Pide cava y anís.*
7. *Están al lado de los vinos.*

Unit 3

About the unit
In this unit pupils will learn to talk and write about feeling well and unwell and to give and receive simple advice about medical matters. They will be able to read and write about maintaining a healthy routine and lifestyle.

New language content:
- parts of the body
- structure with *doler*
- further expressions with *tener*
- structures such as *tener que* + infinitive, *hay que* + infinitive

New contexts:
- ailments, illnesses and remedies
- visiting the doctor, chemist or dentist
- healthy lifestyle

Expectations
At the end of the unit most pupils will be able to: talk about common ailments and symptoms, using a range of expressions; seek advice about remedies; talk, write and understand about aspects of a healthy lifestyle, using new and familiar language from this and previous units.

They should also be able to: work with more complex authentic materials, reading and understanding articles from authentic sources.

Exercise 3.1

A recording of the conversation is available on the CD.

CD 1, track 24

Médico:	Buenos días Jorge.
Jorge:	Buenos días.
Médico:	Hace mucho tiempo que no te veo. ¿Qué tal?
Jorge:	Regular. Últimamente me duele mucho el estómago.
Médico:	¿Desde cuándo?
Jorge:	Hoy es miércoles.....Desde el domingo por la mañana.
Médico:	¿Te duele algo más?
Jorge:	Bueno, la espalda de vez en cuando.
Médico:	Estás un poco más gordo, ¿no? ¿Qué comes?
Jorge:	Como más o menos lo mismo, pero estoy comiendo más hamburguesas y más patatas fritas.
Médico:	¿Y galletas, mantecados, turrón?
Jorge:	Sí, como estamos en Navidad, estoy comiendo muchas de esas cosas, también.
Médico:	¿Y fruta?
Jorge:	No me gusta nada.
Médico:	Tienes que comer fruta, hombre. Es muy buena para la salud. Vamos a tener que cambiar tu dieta.
Jorge:	No doctor, por favor. Cualquier cosa menos eso.
Médico:	Lo siento, Jorge.

Translation:

Médico:	Good Morning Jorge.
Jorge:	Good Morning.
Médico:	I haven't seen you for some time. How are you?
Jorge:	Not too great. I've had stomach ache recently.
Médico:	For some time?
Jorge:	Today's Wednesday. Since Sunday morning.
Médico:	Any other problems?
Jorge:	Well, my back hurts every now and then.
Médico:	You've put on a bit of weight haven't you? What are you eating?
Jorge:	More or less the same things, but I'm eating more hamburgers and chips.
Médico:	And biscuits, *mantecados*, nougat?
Jorge:	Yes, as it's Christmas, I've been eating lots of all those too.
Médico:	How about fruit?
Jorge:	I don't like it at all.
Médico:	But you must eat fruit. It's really good for one's health. We're going to have to change what you eat.
Jorge:	No doctor, please. Anything but that.
Médico:	I'm sorry Jorge.

Answers to questions:
1. Le duele el estómago y, de vez en cuando, la espalda.
2. Desde hace tres días.
3. Dice que está más gordo.
4. Está comiendo más hamburguesas y patatas fritas.
5. Porque es Navidad.
6. Porque es muy buena para la salud.

Translations:
1. His stomach hurts and his back aches from time to time.
2. For 3 days.
3. He says he's put on weight.
4. He's eating more hamburgers and chips.
5. Because it's Christmas.
6. Because it's very good for one's health.

Suggestions: Prior to doing the exercise, pupils should be familiar with the main parts of the body. They could be asked questions beforehand such as *¿Qué es esto?* with the teacher pointing to different parts of his/her body in turn. There is also scope to consider in more detail the structure *hace…..que*. Pupils could be asked to invent sentences using this structure, e.g. *hace dos años que estudiamos español*.

Exercise 3.2
Answers to exercise:
1. *Me duelen los pies.*
2. *¿Te duele la cabeza?*
3. *Les duelen las piernas.*
4. *Nos duelen las manos.*
5. *Le duele la rodilla.*

Suggestions: This exercise may cause some problems (hence the examples in pupils' book) and it would be worth reinforcing the use of the verb by setting them some more sentences like these to translate. Once pupils have grasped the concept, they could be asked to invent and then read out sentences of their own. These could be used for further oral work.

Exercise 3.3
CD 1, track 25
Transcript:

Médico:	*Buenos días, Carmen. ¿Qué te pasa?*
Carmen:	*No me encuentro bien. Me duele todo.*
Médico:	*A ver qué síntomas tienes. ¿Te duele la cabeza?*
Carmen:	*Sí, mucho. Y la garganta también, y la espalda. Y el estómago.*
Médico:	*¿Te duele algo más?*
Carmen:	*Sí, tengo dolor de cuello también.*
Médico:	*¡Madre mía! ¿Cuánto tiempo hace que te sientes así?*
Carmen:	*Desde el fin de semana. Desde la tarde de la paella.*
Médico:	*A lo mejor puede ser de la comida, o puede ser un virus. A ver, échate aquí. Abre la boca….. Tienes la garganta inflamada. Voy a ponerte el termómetro.*
Carmen:	*¿Tengo fiebre?*
Médico:	*Un momento…..Sí, tienes fiebre, no mucha, pero algo tienes.*
Carmen:	*¿Qué puedo hacer?*
Médico:	*Te voy a dar unos antibióticos. Hay que tomar una pastilla tres veces al día con la comida. Y una cosa muy importante: nada de alcohol.*
Carmen:	*Muchas gracias.*
Médico:	*De nada.*

Translation:

Médico:	Good Morning Carmen. What appears to be the problem?
Carmen:	I don't feel well. I ache everywhere.
Médico:	Let's see what your symptoms are. Do you have a headache?
Carmen:	Yes, a bad one. And my throat hurts too and my back. And my tummy.
Médico:	Any aches anywhere else?
Carmen:	Yes, my neck hurts too.
Médico:	Good Lord! How long have you been feeling like this for?
Carmen:	Since last weekend. Since the afternoon when we had *paella*.
Médico:	It might be something you ate, or it might be a virus. Let's see, lie down here. Open your mouth. There's an inflammation on your throat. I'm going to get a thermometer.
Carmen:	Do I have a temperature?
Médico:	Just a moment.....Yes, you've got a temperature, not a really high one, but higher than normal.
Carmen:	What can I do?
Médico:	I'm going to give you some antibiotics. You have to take a pill three times a day with food. And one really important point: no alcohol.
Carmen:	Many thanks.
Médico:	You're welcome.

Questions:
1. *¿Qué le duele a Carmen en particular?*
2. *¿Desde cuando se siente así?*
3. *¿Cuál puede ser la causa, según el médico?*
4. *¿Qué medicamento le da el médico a Carmen?*
5. *¿Cuándo tiene que tomar el medicamento?*
6. *¿Qué dice el médico sobre el alcohol?*

Answers:
1. *Le duelen la cabeza, la garganta, la espalda, el estómago y el cuello.*
2. *Desde el fin de semana/la tarde de la paella.*
3. *O la comida o un virus.*
4. *Le da antibióticos.*
5. *Tres veces al día con la comida.*
6. *No puede tomar alcohol.*

Exercise 3.4

Answers to exercise:
1. *habla*
2. *come*
3. *bebe*
4. *duerme*

Suggestions: Using words such as *come* and *bebe*, pupils could be encouraged to invent some sentences of their own. These sentences should relate in some way to *La salud*, for example *bebe más agua* or *come más verduras*.

Exercise 3.5

Role play.

Exercise 3.6

A recording of the conversation is available on the CD.

CD 1, track 26

Dentista:	Hola Elena. Tanto tiempo sin verte. ¿Te pasa algo?
Elena:	Sí, me duele mucho este diente, aquí, a la derecha.
Dentista:	Abre la boca bien, por favor……….Ah sí, esta muela de aquí. ¿Con qué frecuencia te lavas los dientes?
Elena:	Siempre me los lavo por la mañana después de desayunar, y, por la noche, antes de acostarme.
Dentista:	¿Usas hilo dental?
Elena:	No.
Dentista:	Pues, hay que hacerlo. El hilo dental está muy bien para evitar la formación de caries. Úsalo por la mañana y por la noche, y compra un enjuague también. La higiene bucal es muy importante. ¿Tienes una dieta sana?
Elena:	Bastante, pero me gustan mucho las galletas y las chucherías.
Dentista:	Tienes que comer menos cosas dulces. El azúcar perjudica mucho la dentadura.
Elena:	Vale. ¿Y qué hacemos con este diente, entonces?
Dentista:	Hay que empastarlo.
Elena:	Eso me va a doler mucho, ¿no?
Dentista:	No. Te pongo anestesia local. No te va a doler nada. Pero tienes que tener más cuidado con los dientes. Y hay que venir más de una vez cada tres años.

Translation:

Dentista:	Hello Elena. Long time no see. Do you have a problem?
Elena:	Yes, this tooth here on the right is really hurting.
Dentista:	Open your mouth wide please…..Oh yes, this molar here. How often do you clean your teeth?
Elena:	I always clean them in the morning after breakfast and at night before going to bed.
Dentista:	Do you use dental floss?
Elena:	No.
Dentista:	Well, you must do it. Floss is really good for preventing plaque. Use it in the morning and at night and buy some mouthwash also. Oral hygiene is very important. Do you eat healthily?
Elena:	Pretty much, but I really like biscuits and sweets.
Dentista:	You have to eat less sweet food. Sugar is really bad for your teeth.
Elena:	All right. So, what should we do with this tooth?
Dentista:	It will have to be filled.
Elena:	That's going to hurt a lot isn't it?
Dentista:	No. I'll give you a local anaesthetic. You won't feel a thing. But you must take more care with your teeth. And you must come more than once every three years.

Answers to questions:
1. *Porque le duele el diente.*
2. *Se los lava dos veces al día.*
3. *Para evitar la formación de caries.*
4. *Le dice que tiene que usar enjuague y comer menos cosas dulces.*
5. *Lo va a empastar.*
6. *Porque le va a poner una anestesia local.*
7. *Tiene que ir al dentista con más frecuencia.*

Translations:
1. Because she's got toothache.
2. She cleans them twice a day.
3. Because it's good for preventing plaque.
4. He says she has to use mouthwash and eat less sweet things.
5. He's going to put a filling on it.
6. As he's going to give her a local anaesthetic.
7. She has to go to the dentist more often.

Exercise 3.7

Translation:

Dear Susana

I am writing to you to ask your help about a problem that I've had for quite some time. The problem is that I'm putting on more and more weight and I don't know what to do. I try to do a bit of exercise and not to eat too many fatty foods, like sweet things and crisps. I also go on diets often. I go to the swimming pool every now and then and go jogging once a month. I eat quite a lot of fruit and salads, but I really like bread and biscuits, and especially chocolate. I don't usually have much breakfast, nor do I eat much at lunchtime, and so I often stuff myself at night. I try not to have a lot of alcohol, but I love beer. I also like coca-cola. I wonder if you can tell me what I have to do to lose weight rather than put it on so much.

Love

Ana

1. *Porque está gorda y quiere ayuda.*
2. *Hace un poco de ejercicio, intenta no comer demasiada comida grasa e intenta no beber mucho alcohol.*
3. *No desayuna mucho, tampoco como mucho al mediodía.*
4. *Le gustan la cerveza y la coca-cola.*

Translations:
1. Because she's overweight and wants help.
2. She does a little bit of exercise, tries not to eat too much fatty food and tries not to drink too much alcohol.
3. She doesn't eat much breakfast, nor does she eat very much for lunch.
4. She likes beer and coca-cola.

Suggestions: As usual, the text gives scope for additional oral work. One could probe deeper about the type of exercise Ana does, and how often, and be more specific about her diet.

Homework: Either for prep, or for additional classwork, pupils could be asked to write their own letter to an agony aunt. This could be used for oral work as pupils read out their accounts to the rest of the class.

Exercise 3.9

A recording of the conversation is available on the CD.

CD 1, track 27

Farmacéutico: *Buenos días señora. ¿En qué puedo ayudarle?*
María: *Tengo un dolor de cabeza tremendo. Me encuentro fatal.*
Farmacéutico: *Siéntese, por favor. Tome, aquí tiene usted una silla.*
María: *Muchas gracias.*
Farmacéutico: *De nada. ¿Le duele algo más?*
María: *No, solamente la cabeza, pero me duele muchísimo. Demasiado vino anoche.*
Farmacéutico: *Bueno, espere unos segundos. Le voy a dar unas pastillas…..Tome una, dos veces al día, con la comida. Descanse mucho, beba mucha agua, y coma algo ligero.*

Translation:
Farmacéutico: Good Morning, Madam. How can I help you?
María: I've got an awful headache. I feel terrible.
Farmacéutico: Please sit down. Here, take this chair.
María: Many thanks.
Farmacéutico: You're welcome. Do you have any other aches or pains?
María: No, just a headache, but it's really bad. Too much wine last night.
Farmacéutico: Well, wait a few seconds. I'm going to give you some pills…Take one twice a day with food. Rest a lot, drink lots of water and eat something light.

Answers to exercise:
Siéntese
Tome
Espere
Tome
Descanse
Beba
Coma

Suggestions: Once the various imperatives have been identified, it should be verified that pupils have recognised the pattern, i.e. *-ar* verbs end in an *e* while *–er* verbs end in an *a*. One would also want to point out that the same applies to *–ir* verbs.

Exercise 3.10

A recording of the suggested amended conversation is available on the CD.

CD 1, track 28

Answers to exercise (in bold):
Farmacéutico: *Buenos días **María**. ¿En qué puedo ayuda**rte**?*
María: *Tengo un dolor de cabeza tremendo. Me encuentro fatal.*
Farmacéutico: ***Siéntate** por favor. **Toma**, aquí **tienes** una silla.*
María: *Muchas gracias.*
Farmacéutico: *De nada. ¿**Te** duele algo más?*
María: *No, solamente la cabeza, pero me duele muchísimo. Demasiado vino anoche.*
Farmacéutico: *Bueno, **espera** unos segundos. **Te** voy a dar unas pastillas…..**Toma** una dos veces al día con la comida. **Descansa** mucho, **bebe** mucha agua, y **come** algo ligero.*

Exercise 3.11

Translation:

Dear Ana

Many thanks for your letter. First of all, I have to tell you that you mustn't worry too much. Of course it's important to look after the way one looks, and health is very important, but it's also important not to let your physical appearance become an obsession. That said, let's see if we can be of help. As you recognise in your letter, one has to exercise and I think that you should try to go to the swimming pool more often. Besides, instead of going for a jog once a month, you need to try to do it more often. One has to make a mental effort, not just a physical one. Also, there are other ways of getting fit. Cycling, for example, is really good, and is not harmful to one's body.

As regards food, it's really good to eat fruit and salads, but you must eat less bread, biscuits and chocolate. They make you put on weight. You must also change your eating habits. Breakfast is the most important meal and so you must make an effort to eat more in the morning. You also need to eat well at lunchtime. The body needs energy and food is essential for that. Besides, if you eat more during the day, you won't have to stuff yourself at night, something which is very bad for your health.

At the end of the day, it shouldn't be an obsession, but there are several things which you should try to change.

Lots of love

Susana

Answers to questions:
1. *Dice que no debe preocuparse.*
2. *Dice que tiene que intentar hacerlo más.*
3. *Porque no perjudica al cuerpo.*
4. *Dice que está bien comer fruta y ensalada, pero tiene que comer menos pan, galletas y chocolate.*
5. *Porque el cuerpo necesita energía y, además, no va a tener que inflarse por la noche.*
6. *Parece ser muy simpática porque reconoce las cosas buenas que hace Ana, y quiere ayudarla.*

Translations:

1. She says she mustn't worry.
2. She says she must try to do more.
3. Because it doesn't harm the body.
4. She says it's good to eat fruit and salad, but she has to eat less bread, biscuits and chocolate.
5. As the body needs energy and also she won't have to stuff herself in the evenings.
6. She seems really nice as she acknowledges the good things Ana does, but she also wants to help her.

Exercise 3.12

Suggestions: There is good scope for oral work here. Pupils should be encouraged to read out individual pieces of advice in terms of what people should and should not do. Questions can then be put to others in the class about what has been said and whether it is good advice or not.

Exercise 3.13

Answers to questions:
1. *Libra, porque le va a doler todo y va a tener mucha fiebre.*
2. *Aries, porque tiene que hacer más ejercicio.*
3. *Tauro, Leo, Escorpio y Capricornio.*
4. *Libra, porque va a perderlo.*

Translations:
1. Libra, as he/she will be in pain everywhere and he/she'll have a temperature.
2. Aries, because he/she has to do more exercise.
3. Taurus, Leo, Scorpio and Capricorn.
4. Libra, as he/she is going to lose his/her job.

Homework/classwork: Pupils could be asked to draw up their own horoscopes.

Exercise 3.14
CD 1, track 29
Transcript:

Carlos: *A mí me gusta mantenerme en forma. Por eso procuro tener cuidado con lo que como. Yo creo que es importante tener una dieta equilibrada. Por lo tanto como carne, pescado, verduras y mucha fruta. Me gusta mucho el sabor de los plátanos y dicen que es una cosa muy sana. Por supuesto, también me gustan las patatas fritas y el chocolate, pero no los como mucho. Además, me gusta hacer ejercicio, así que no pasa nada. Mi punto débil es el helado. Me encanta y no puedo resistirlo. Me gusta mucho el zumo de naranja y siempre bebo mucha agua.*

Los deportes me encantan, y son una forma fantástica de mantenerse en forma. Juego al baloncesto tres veces a la semana, y al fútbol todos los sábados. También me gusta mucho el ciclismo y doy una vuelta en bici todos los días después del colegio. En el futuro me gustaría jugar más al tenis. Es un deporte que me gusta mucho pero no tengo bastante tiempo para practicarlo.

Otra cosa que me parece muy importante es dormir. Mi madre dice que duermo demasiado, pero yo necesito dormir más de ocho horas para sentirme bien.

Translation:

Carlos: I like keeping in shape. For that reason I try to take care about what I eat. I think it's important to have a balanced diet. Therefore I eat meat, fish, vegetables and a lot of fruit. I really like the taste of bananas and people say it's really healthy. Of course, I also like crisps and chocolate, but I don't eat them too much. Besides, I like doing a lot of exercise, so it's no big deal. My weak point is ice-cream. I love it and can't resist it. I love orange juice and I always drink a lot of water.

I love sports and they're a fantastic way of keeping fit. I play basketball three times a week and I always play football on Saturdays. I also really like cycling and I go for a ride every day after school. In the future I'd like to play more tennis. It's a sport that I like a lot, but I don't have much time to play.

Something else that I think is really important is sleep. My mother says I sleep too much, but I need to sleep more than eight hours to feel good.

CD 1, track 30

María: *Yo no suelo tener demasiado cuidado con la comida porque no suelo engordar. Puedo inflarme de galletas y chucherías y no pasa nada. Dicho esto, también me gusta la comida sana. Me encanta el pescado, sobre todo el marisco como las gambas y los mejillones. También procuro tomar fruta. Las naranjas y la piña me gustan bastante. Hay una cosa mala que no puedo evitar: el tabaco. Fumo casi una cajetilla diaria y esto me preocupa. Por lo menos no bebo mucho alcohol, solamente una cerveza de vez en cuando.*

No soy muy deportista, pero reconozco que la salud es importante e intento hacer ejercicio de vez en cuando. Subo todos los domingos a la Sierra para esquiar y voy a la piscina una vez a la semana. En el futuro, voy a aprender a jugar al golf; Sergio García me encanta.

Otra cosa que me resulta importante es descansar. El trabajo es importante, pero el cuerpo también necesita un descanso de vez en cuando.

Translation

María: I don't tend to take too much care over what I eat because I don't tend to put on weight. I can stuff myself with biscuits and sweets and there's no problem. Having said that, I also like healthy food. I love fish, especially shellfish like prawns and mussels. I also like to eat fruit. I do like oranges and pineapple. There is one bad thing I can't avoid: tobacco. I smoke almost a packet a day and this worries me. At least I don't drink much alcohol, only a beer every now and then.

I'm not very sporty, but I realise that one's health is important and I try to do some exercise every now and then. I go up to the mountains every Sunday to ski and I go to the swimming pool once a week. In the future I'm going to learn to play golf. I love Sergio García.

Something else that I think is really important is rest. Work's important, but the body needs a rest once in a while.

CD 1, track 31

Carla: *Yo soy vegetariana. No como carne nunca, pero sí pescado. Es muy bueno para la salud. Me encantan las ensaladas, sobre todo si llevan tomates. Tengo un punto débil con la comida: las galletas de chocolate. Son una obsesión. Voy a intentar comer menos. En cuanto a la bebida, me gusta mucho la coca-cola. También me apetece una copa de vino tinto de vez en cuando.*

El deporte que más me gusta es la gimnasia. Voy al gimnasio todos los días después del colegio y así me mantengo en forma. También disfruto mucho. Durante las vacaciones vamos a una casita que tenemos en el campo. Allí monto a caballo y en bicicleta.

Otras cosas que me gusta hacer son leer y escribir. Así me relajo mucho. Yo creo que la salud mental es tan importante como la salud física.

Translation

Carla: I'm a vegetarian. I don't eat meat, but I do eat fish. It's very good for one's health. I love salads, especially if they have tomatoes in them. I have one weak spot where food's concerned: chocolate biscuits. They're an obsession. I'm going to try to eat less. As for drink, I really like coca-cola. I also like to have a glass of red wine every now and then.

The sport I like most is gymnastics. I go to the gym every day after school and that's how I keep fit. I also really enjoy it. In the holidays we go to a little house we have in the country. I go riding there – on horseback and on my bike.

Other things I like to do are reading and writing. That's how I get to really relax. I think that one's mental health is just as important as one's physical health.

Questions for each:
1. ¿Qué le gusta comer?
2. ¿Cuál es su punto débil?
3. ¿Qué le gusta beber?
4. ¿Qué deportes le gustan?
5. ¿Cuántas veces los practica?
6. ¿Qué quiere hacer en el futuro?
7. ¿Qué otras cosas le parecen importantes?

Answers for Carlos:
1. *Carne, pescado, verduras, fruta, patatas fritas y chocolate.*
2. *El helado.*
3. *El zumo de naranja y agua.*
4. *El baloncesto, el fútbol y el ciclismo.*
5. *Juega al baloncesto tres veces a la semana, al fútbol los sábados y monta en bici todos los días.*
6. *Jugar más al tenis.*
7. *Dormir.*

Answers for María:
1. *Las galletas, la fruta (naranja, piña), las "chuches", el pescado, el marisco (gambas y mejillones).*
2. *El tabaco.*
3. *La cerveza.*
4. *Esquiar, nadar.*
5. *Esquia todos los domingos y nada una vez a la semana.*
6. *Jugar al golf.*
7. *Descansar.*

Answers for Carla:
1. *El pescado, la ensalada, los tomates.*
2. *Las galletas de chocolate.*
3. *La coca-cola y una copa de vino tinto de vez en cuando.*
4. *La gimnasia, montar a caballo/en bicicleta.*
5. *Hace gimnasia todos los días, y monta a caballo y en bicicleta durante las vacaciones.*
6. *No dice nada sobre el futuro.*
7. *Leer y escribir.*

Suggestions: After clarifying the answers to the questions as far as each of the three speakers is concerned, pupils could be asked to provide their own account. This could be structured in the same way as Carlos, María, Carla. Individual accounts could then be read out and used for further listening and oral work. There may be scope here to make comparisons incorporating structures that have previously been learned, e.g. *más .... que, menos .... que.* For example, a pupil might say '*yo soy más deportista que María*'. More general comparisons could also be made in terms of differences in lifestyle. For example, one could say '*la gente usa mucho más aceite en España*' or '*se juega más al baloncesto en España*'. There is also an opportunity to reinforce the compound future. Pupils might be asked about what they are going to do to improve their health. This would clearly trigger the response '*voy a ......*'.

Exercise 3.15

Translation

DRUG ADDICTION: NATIONAL PLAN TO COMBAT DRUG PROBLEM

According to a survey, 78% of Spanish adolescents consume alcohol and 20% smoke each day.

Alcohol and tobacco are habitual drugs for Spanish students between the ages of 14 and 18. According to the first survey of adolescents for the "Plan Nacional sobre Drogas" (PNSD), 78.5% admit to drinking alcohol, and of those 95.4% do it at the weekend. 20% smoke on a daily basis, with an average of 9 cigarettes a day. As far as other drugs are concerned, the main one is hashish (12% a month). The substances they most fear are heroin and cocaine, although the risk perceived is more to do with the quantity consumed rather than the drugs themselves.

Two legal drugs, alcohol and tobacco, are the ones most consumed by Spanish adolescents, according to a PNSD survey carried out towards the end of 1994 amongst 21,094 students in 395 secondary schools in the public and private sector.

Boys drink more: 14.2%, on more than two occasions a week, compared with 6.2% of girls. This consumption takes place virtually exclusively at the weekend (95.4%). Beer is the most popular drink, and wine on a more sporadic basis. 38.6% of 14 and 15 year-olds drink in discotheques, and 56%, in bars, a statistic that shows that many bars ignore, with no fear of reprisal, the law that stipulates alcohol must not be sold to the under-age.

'It's not something that is prohibited in theory,' said Carlos López Riaño, the Government representative for the PNSD, on presenting the survey with Álvaro Marchesi, the Secretary of State for Education. 'It is clearly illegal. Bar owners and the like have to sit down with the Establishment and citizens' organizations to work out solutions. We can't have one municipality working to the letter of the law whilst another ignores it. And the family is an entity that is increasingly important in dealing with the problem.'

On announcing that these surveys will now happen on a yearly basis, Marchesi and Carlos López Riaño reflected that 'fortunately this drug consumption is not happening within the school environment,' although López Riaño added that 'what goes on beyond the school gates is an entirely different matter.' Consumption of any drug increases with age. For example, as regards alcohol, the figure for those who drink on a weekly basis increases from 17.3% for 14 year-olds to as much as 54.4% for 18 year-olds. 43.5% of those interviewed have been drunk at some point, 24.5 of whom have been so within the last month.

Tobacco is also common amongst them. The majority of young smokers who smoke on a daily basis consume between 6 to 10 cigarettes a day, with an average of 9.2%. Age is a key factor: at 14, 8.1% smoke daily, but at 18, this figure rises to 36.2%: also the figure rises from 7 cigarettes a day to 11.4. There are more girls who smoke on a daily basis than boys: 24.1% compared with 17.1%. 32.9% of girls state that they have smoked within the last month compared with 23.4% for the boys. However, with regard to the numbers who consume half a packet a day, 35.4% are boys 20.3% are girls. The average age for when youngsters start smoking is between 13 and 14.

Apart from alcohol and tobacco, the most widely-consumed drug is hashish (Cannabis): 12.2% of secondary school pupils state that they have consumed it at some point in the last month.

Answers to exercise:
1. D
2. F
3. H
4. B
5. E
6. J
7. A
8. G
9. C
10. I

Suggestions: There are other percentages in the text that have not been used and pupils could be asked to write down in Spanish what these other percentages refer to. Clearly, depending on their level, they could either be instructed to use the words in the text, or encouraged to try to use their own words.

Exercise 3.16

Translation:

Dear Susana,

Many thanks for your letter and for your advice. I'm doing a lot more exercise now and I'm also eating a lot better. First, I'm jogging every day before going to school and after eating a bigger breakfast. I go to the swimming pool three times a week. In addition, I've got a new bike and I go out for a ride three or four times a week. I weigh six kilos less.

I don't eat any more biscuits or chocolate. I eat bread, but only with meals. I eat well in the morning and at lunchtime and a lot less at night. I think I look prettier as Juan, the best looking boy in the class takes a lot more notice of me – not like before. I'm really happy.

Love

Ana

Answers to exercise:
1. *Hace footing todos los días antes del colegio y va a la piscina tres veces a la semana. También da una vuelta en bici tres o cuatro veces a la semana.*
2. *Ya no come ni galletas ni chocolate. Come bastante más por la mañana y a mediodía, y menos por la noche.*
3. *Pesa seis kilos menos.*
4. *Porque ahora el chico más guapo de la clase se fija en ella.*

Translations:
1. She goes jogging every day before school and goes to the pool 3 times a week. She also goes for a bike ride 3 or 4 times a week.
2. She doesn't eat any more biscuits or chocolate. She eats a lot more in the morning and at lunchtime and less at night.
3. She weighs 6 kilos less.
4. Because now the best-looking boy in the class takes notice of her.

Exercise 3.17
CD 1, track 32

Transcript:

Médico:	Buenos días Jorge. ¿Qué tal?
Jorge:	Tirando. La nueva dieta no me gusta mucho. No entiendo por qué tengo que comer todas estas cosas raras.
Médico:	¿Qué cosas raras?
Jorge:	Cereales, fruta, verduras, ensalada. Si comemos para tener energía, ¿qué importa si como hamburguesas en lugar de toda esa comida tan rara?
Médico:	Es importante hacer una dieta equilibrada.
Jorge:	¿Por qué?
Médico:	Porque el cuerpo necesita diferentes vitaminas, proteínas y minerales. Las hamburguesas tienen algunas cosas buenas, pero otras no. Por ejemplo, los cereales suelen tener B vitaminas y son muy importantes para tu concentración. También tienen fibra, proteínas y hierro. El hierro es muy bueno para tu energía.
Jorge:	La verdad es que me encuentro un poco mejor. Peso un poco menos.
Médico:	¿Y cómo estás del dolor de la espalda?
Jorge:	Igual. Me duele de vez en cuando. ¿Por qué?
Médico:	Siento decírtelo, pero todavía estás un poco gordo, y eso no es bueno para la espalda. ¿Estás haciendo más ejercicio?
Jorge:	Sí, un poco. Voy a la piscina dos o tres veces a la semana y nado una hora. También hago footing los fines de semana.
Médico:	Eso está bien, pero también tienes que desarrollar los músculos abdominales.
Jorge:	¿Qué significa eso?
Médico:	Necesitas tener el estómago más musculoso y menos gordo. Eso es muy bueno para la espalda. Hay que hacer treinta o cuarenta ejercicios abdominales todos los días y así la espalda no te va a doler tanto.

Translation:

Médico:	Good Morning Jorge. How's it going?
Jorge:	So-so. I'm not too fond of the new diet. I don't understand why I have to eat all these strange things.
Médico:	What strange things?
Jorge:	Cereal, fruit, vegetables, salad. If we eat to get energy, what does it matter if I eat hamburgers instead of all that really strange food?
Médico:	It's important to have a balanced diet.
Jorge:	Why?
Médico:	Because the body needs different vitamins, proteins, and minerals. Hamburgers have some good things, but not others. For example, cereals usually have a lot of B vitamins and they are really good for your concentration. They also have fibre, proteins and iron. Iron is very good for your energy.

Jorge:	The truth is I do feel a bit better. I've lost a bit of weight.
Médico:	And how's your back?
Jorge:	The same. It hurts from time to time. Why is that?
Médico:	I'm sorry to have to tell you this, but you're still a little overweight, and that's not good for your back. Are you doing more exercise?
Jorge:	A little bit. I go to the swimming-pool two or three times a week and I swim for an hour. I also go jogging on the weekends.
Médico:	That's good, but you also have to develop your abdominal muscles.
Jorge:	What's that mean?
Médico:	You need your stomach to be more muscular and less fat. That's really good for one's back. You have to do thirty or forty sit-ups every day and then your back won't hurt so much.

Questions:
1. *¿Cuál es la nueva dieta de Jorge?*
2. *¿Qué necesita el cuerpo?*
3. *¿Qué ejercicio hace Jorge ahora?*
4. *¿Qué tiene que hacer Jorge para la espalda?*

Answers:
1. *Cereales, fruta, verduras, ensalada.*
2. *Necesita vitaminas, proteínas y minerales.*
3. *Va a la piscina dos o tres veces a la semana, y hace footing los fines de semana.*
4. *Tiene que hacer ejercicios abdominales todos los días.*

Exercise 3.18

Suggestions: Pupils should be encouraged to read out their accounts. Notes should be taken by the rest with a view to being able to answer teacher-led questions afterwards. This exercise could lead onto another: pupils could be asked to choose a famous person, e.g. Michael Owen, and the class could be asked to speculate as to his or her diet.

Unit 4

About the unit
In this unit pupils will learn about shopping, in particular shopping for clothes. They will learn about describing clothes and giving opinions and preferences.

New language content:
- expressions of size
- demonstrative adjectives and pronouns (*este, ese, aquel*)
- use of interrogative *¿Cuál?*

New contexts:
- shopping for clothes and presents
- discussion of fashions
- consideration of appropriateness of clothes

Expectations
At the end of this unit most pupils will be able to: perform role-plays to buy items in shops, stating colour, size and preference, using demonstrative adjectives and pronouns to point out items; describe a choice of clothing for a particular event and say why it is or is not appropriate.

They should also be able to: comprehend, speak and write about more complex situations involving shopping and preferences for clothes.

La ropa
This unit should begin with teachers reinforcing the pronunciation of the different clothes worn by Jorge and Lucía at the beginning of the unit in the pupils' book. This can be done in either of the following ways:

1. Via the whiteboard, pointing to individual items, and asking *¿Qué es esto?*
2. By asking a series of questions using *¿Cómo se dice...?* E.g. *¿Cómo se dice* the trousers *en español?*

Exercise 4.1
CD 2, track 1

Transcript:

Paco:	Bueno, ¿qué quieres regalarle a tu novia para su cumpleaños?
Julio:	Ropa. A Regina le gusta mucho la ropa.
Paco:	¿Por qué no le compras un CD?
Julio:	¿Por qué?
Paco:	Porque no es tan caro. La ropa cuesta mucho.
Julio:	Depende. Hay una tienda en la calle Paz que tiene una ropa muy chula y más barata que en los grandes almacenes. Se llama "Adolfo López".
Paco:	¿Qué tipo de ropa le gusta?
Julio:	¡Paco, mi novia es una chica!
Paco:	¡Menos mal!
Julio:	Quiero decir que le gusta todo.
Paco:	Sí, pero ¿qué, en particular?
Julio:	Los vaqueros, las faldas, los vestidos, y, sobre todo, los zapatos. A Regina le encantan los zapatos.
Paco:	¿Y por qué no vas a "Zara"? Está de rebajas y hay unas gangas impresionantes. Además tienen unos zapatos chulísimos para chicas.
Julio:	¿Cómo lo sabes?
Paco:	Entré el otro día. Tengo que regalarle algo a Inés, también.
Julio:	¿Quién es Inés?
Paco:	Mi nueva novia. A ella también le encanta la ropa.
Julio:	¿Qué vas a regalarle?
Paco:	Una minifalda.
Julio:	¿Para tí o para ella?
Paco:	Para los dos.

Translation:

Paco:	Well, what are you going to give your girlfriend for her birthday?
Julio:	Clothes. Regina really likes clothes.
Paco:	Why don't you buy her a CD?
Julio:	Why?
Paco:	Because it's not so expensive. Clothes cost a lot.
Julio:	It depends. There's a shop in Paz Street which has really cool clothes and they're a lot cheaper than in department stores. It's called "Adolfo López".
Paco:	What type of clothes does she like?
Julio:	Paco, my girlfriend's female!
Paco:	Thank God for that!
Julio:	I mean that she likes everything.
Paco:	Yes, but what in particular?
Julio:	Jeans, skirts, dresses and especially shoes. Regina loves shoes.
Paco:	Why don't you go to Zara? There's a sale on and there are some amazing bargains. Besides, they have some really cool shoes for girls.
Julio:	How do you know?
Paco:	I went in the other day. I've got to buy something for Inés too.
Julio:	Who's Inés?
Paco:	My new girlfriend. She also loves clothes.
Julio:	What are you going to give her?
Paco:	A miniskirt.
Julio:	Is that for you or for her?
Paco:	For both of us.

Questions:
1. ¿Por qué Paco dice que un CD es mejor que la ropa?
2. ¿Por qué le gusta a Julio la tienda en la calle Paz?
3. ¿Cómo se llaman las novias de Julio y de Paco?
4. ¿Qué ropa, en particular, le gusta a la novia de Julio?
5. ¿Por qué es una buena idea ir a Zara?
6. ¿Qué va a regalarle Paco a su novia?

Answers:
1. Porque no es tan caro/cuesta menos.
2. Porque la ropa allí es muy chula y es más barata que en los almacenes.
3. La de Julio se llama Regina y la de Paco se llama Inés.
4. Le gustan los vaqueros, las faldas, los vestidos, y sobre todo los zapatos.
5. Está de rebajas y hay unas gangas impresionantes.
6. Una minifalda.

Exercise 4.2

A recording of the conversation is available on the CD.

CD 2, track 2

Dependienta:	¿Puedo ayudarte?
Julio:	Sí, me gustan mucho estos zapatos. ¿Qué valen?
Dependienta:	¿Cuáles? ¿Estos blancos?
Julio:	No. Estos rojos de aquí.
Dependienta:	Los blancos cuestan menos que los rojos porque están de rebajas, y los rojos no.
Julio:	¿Qué valen?
Dependienta:	Los rojos valen 60 euros, y los blancos, 45.
Julio:	Son un poco caros, ¿no?
Dependienta:	Es una marca muy buena.
Julio:	Y este pantalón de aquí, ¿Qué vale?
Dependienta:	¿Cuál? ¿Éste? ......45 euros. Es otra marca muy buena.
Julio:	Y esta falda negra, ¿Qué vale?
Dependienta:	35 euros, pero no quedan muchas. ¿Para quién es?
Julio:	Para mi novia.
Dependienta:	¿Y qué talla tiene?
Julio:	La 36, creo. No estoy seguro porque solamente salgo con ella desde hace tres semanas.
Dependienta:	Lo siento mucho, pero no quedan de esa talla.
Julio:	Bueno, me llevo los zapatos blancos.
Dependienta:	¿Qué número calza?
Julio:	El 37.
Dependienta:	Muy bien. Ahora mismo te los traigo.

Translation:

Dependienta:	Can I help you?
Julio:	Yes, I really like these shoes. How much do they cost?
Dependienta:	Which ones? These white ones?
Julio:	No. These red ones here.
Dependienta:	The white ones cost less than the red ones as they're in the sale and the red ones aren't.

Julio:	How much do they cost?
Dependienta:	The red ones cost 60 euros and the white ones 45.
Julio:	That's a bit expensive, isn't it?
Dependienta:	It's a very good make.
Julio:	And these trousers here? How much are they?
Dependienta:	Which ones? These? …….45 euros. It's another really good label.
Julio:	And this black skirt, how much does it cost?
Dependienta:	35 euros, but there aren't many left. Who's it for?
Julio:	For my girlfriend.
Dependienta:	What's her size?
Julio:	36 I think. I'm not sure as we've only been going out for 3 weeks.
Dependienta:	I'm really sorry, but we haven't got any left in that size.
Julio:	OK, I'll take the white shoes.
Dependienta:	What size does she take?
Julio:	37.
Dependienta:	Fine. I'll be right back with them.

Answers to questions:
1. *Porque están de rebajas.*
2. *Cuesta 45 euros.*
3. *Quedan pocas.*
4. *Salen desde hace poco tiempo/3 semanas.*
5. *Compra los zapatos blancos.*

Translations:
1. Because they're in the sale.
2. 45 euros.
3. There are only a few left.
4. They've only been going out for a short time/3 weeks.
5. He buys the white shoes.

Exercise 4.3

Suggestions: Pupils should be asked to enact their dialogue and the rest of the class should then be asked questions about the content.

Exercise 4.4

Suggestions: Pupils could be asked to read out individual sentences. Others could then be asked about what has been said. Furthermore, the sentences could be translated orally.

Exercise 4.5

A recording of the completed dialogue is available on the CD.

CD 2, track 3

Answers to exercise (in bold):

Cliente:	*Quisiera probarme **esta** camisa.*
Dependienta:	*¿**Cuál**? ¿La roja?*
Cliente:	*Sí, y también **este** pantalón.*
Dependienta:	*¿**Cuál**? ¿El negro?*
Cliente:	*No. El verde. Y **estos** zapatos.*
Dependienta:	*¿**Cuáles**? ¿Estos de aquí?*
Cliente:	*Sí.*

Translation:
Cliente:	I'd like to try this shirt on.
Dependienta:	Which one? The red one?
Cliente:	Yes, and this pair of trousers too.
Dependienta:	Which one? The black pair?
Cliente:	No. The green pair. And these shoes.
Dependienta:	Which ones? These ones here?
Cliente:	Yes.

Exercise 4.6

A recording of the dialogue is available on the CD.

CD 2, track 4

Answers to exercise:
- **A:** *Quisiera probarme estos zapatos.*
- **B:** *¿Cuáles?*
- **A:** *Estos negros. Y esta camisa.*
- **B:** *¿Cuál?*
- **A:** *Esta roja.*

Exercise 4.7

Suggestions: As usual, role-plays should be enacted and used for comprehension and oral work.

Exercise 4.8
CD 2, track 5

Transcript:

Pepe:	*¡Dígame!*
Giles:	*Hola Pepe. Soy Giles. Llamo porque mañana llego a Málaga.*
Pepe:	*Ya. Yo voy con mi padre a recogerte. ¿Cuándo llega el avión?*
Giles:	*A las ocho de la tarde. Te llamo porque no sabes cómo soy.*
Pepe:	*Bueno, sé que eres alto, rubio y con los ojos azules.*
Giles:	*Sí, pero me parece que va a haber más personas así en el aeropuerto.*
Pepe:	*Creo que tienes razón. ¿Qué ropa vas a llevar puesta?*
Giles:	*Me voy a poner unos vaqueros negros, una camisa amarilla, y unas zapatillas rojas y blancas. Voy a tener una maleta verde y una mochila naranja de "Nike".*
Pepe:	*Aquí en Málaga hace muy mal tiempo. Hace frío. Deberías ponerte un abrigo o algo así.*
Giles:	*Vale. También me voy a poner una chaqueta negra, de cuero, y una gorra azul de "Nike". ¿Y tú?*
Pepe:	*Yo no tengo nada de moda. Me pongo unos vaqueros normales, una camisa blanca y un anorak azul marino. Si tienes algún problema, llámame al móvil.*
Giles:	*No tengo el número porque mi perro se comió mi agenda. ¿Me lo das otra vez, por favor?*
Pepe:	*Claro. Es el 630 967344. Hasta mañana y ¡buen viaje!*
Giles:	*Gracias. Hasta mañana.*

Translation:
Pepe:	Hello.
Giles:	Hi Pepe. It's Giles. I'm calling because tomorrow I arrive in Málaga.
Pepe:	Yes, I know. I'm going with my father to meet you. When does the plane arrive?
Giles:	At 8 in the evening. I'm calling because you don't know what I look like.

Pepe:	Well, I know you're tall, blond with blue eyes.
Giles:	Yes, but I think there might be a few more people like that in the airport.
Pepe:	I think you're right. What will you be wearing?
Giles:	I'm going to put on some black jeans, a yellow shirt, and some red and white trainers. I'll have a green suitcase and an orange Nike rucksack.
Pepe:	The weather's bad here in Málaga. It's cold. You should wear an overcoat or something.
Giles:	OK. I'll also be wearing a black leather jacket and a blue Nike cap. And you?
Pepe:	I don't have anything trendy. I'll be wearing some normal jeans, a white shirt and a navy blue anorak. If you have any problems, call me on the mobile.
Giles:	I don't have the number as my dog ate my phonebook. Could you give it to me again please?
Pepe:	Sure. It's 630 967344. See you tomorrow and have a good trip!
Giles:	Thanks. See you tomorrow.

Answers to questions:
1. Llega a Málaga a las 8 en avión.
2. Es alto, rubio, con los ojos azules.
3. Va a ponerse unos vaqueros, una camisa amarilla y unas zapatillas rojas y blancas. También se va a poner una chaqueta negra de cuero y un gorro azul de "Nike".
4. Porque hace frío en Málaga.
5. Va a ponerse unos vaqueros, una camisa blanca y un anorak azul.
6. Es el 630 967344.

Translations:
1. He arrives at Málaga at 8 by plane.
2. He's tall, blond with blue eyes.
3. He's going to wear some black jeans, a yellow shirt, some red and white trainers. He's also going to wear a black leather jacket and a blue Nike cap.
4. Because it's cold in Málaga.
5. He'll be wearing jeans, a white shirt and a blue anorak.
6. It's 630 967344.

Exercise 4.9

Suggestions: Dialogues should be enacted and used for comprehension and oral work.

Exercise 4.10

A recording of the conversation is available on the CD.

CD 2, track 6

Policía:	Dígame señor.
Turista:	Hay unos tipos bastante sospechosos en la playa.
Policía:	¿Por qué sospechosos?
Turista:	Creo que son ladrones. Están mirando los bolsos y las mochilas de la gente en la playa.
Policía:	¿Cuántos son?
Turista:	Hay tres.
Policía:	¿Y cómo son?
Turista:	Hay uno un poco gordo. Lleva un pantalón corto, unas sandalias y una camiseta polo.

Policía:	¿De qué color?
Turista:	No estoy seguro porque estoy muy nervioso.
Policía:	¿Y los otros?
Turista:	El segundo lleva un pantalón de chándal, una camiseta y unas zapatillas muy viejas y sucias. El tercero lleva un bañador, una camiseta polo, unas chanclas, y un sombrero. Todos tienen gafas de sol.
Policía:	Muy bien. Gracias, señor.
Turista:	¿Qué va a hacer?
Policía:	Ahora no podemos hacer nada porque ha habido un accidente de tráfico muy grande en la autovía y no puedo mandar a nadie, de momento.

Translation:

Policía:	How can I help you sir?
Turista:	There are some rather suspicious-looking characters on the beach.
Policía:	Why suspicious?
Turista:	I think they're thieves. They're looking at the bags and rucksacks of the people on the beach.
Policía:	How many of them are there?
Turista:	Three.
Policía:	And what do they look like?
Turista:	One of them's a bit fat. He's wearing shorts, sandals and a short-sleeved sports shirt.
Policía:	What colour?
Turista:	I'm not sure as I am rather nervous.
Policía:	And the others?
Turista:	The second one is wearing tracksuit bottoms, a T-shirt and some old, dirty trainers. The third's wearing a swimming costume, a short-sleeved sports shirt, some flip-flops and a hat. They're all wearing sunglasses.
Policía:	Very well. Thank you sir.
Turista:	What are you going to do?
Policía:	We can't do anything now as there's been a big traffic accident on the motorway and I can't send anybody for the time being.

Answers to questions:
1. *Porque están mirando los bolsos y las mochilas de la gente en la playa.*
2. *Porque está muy nervioso.*
3. *Son viejas y sucias.*
4. *Todos llevan gafas de sol.*
5. *A causa de un accidente de tráfico.*

Translations:
1. Because they're looking at the bags and rucksacks of the people on the beach.
2. Because he is very nervous.
3. They are old and dirty.
4. They are all wearing sunglasses.
5. Because of a traffic accident.

Exercise 4.12

A recording of the completed conversation is available on the CD.

CD 2, track 7

Answers to exercise (in bold):

Elena:	¿Te gusta **esa** camisa?
Jorge:	¿**Cuál**? ¿La verde?
Elena:	Sí.
Jorge:	No. Pero me gusta **ese** chándal.
Elena:	¿**Cuál**? ¿El negro? Es un **poco** hortera, ¿no?
Jorge:	No. El negro está muy de **moda**.
Elena:	Y **esos** zapatos. ¿Te gustan?
Jorge:	No, pero me gustan **esas** botas.
Elena:	¿**Cuáles**? ¿**Ésas**? Son muy feas.
Jorge:	No. Son **fantásticas**.
Elena:	Jorge, ¡qué hortera **eres**!

(Translation provided as part of Exercise 4.13)

Exercise 4.13

Translation:

Elena:	Do you like that shirt?
Jorge:	Which one? The green one?
Elena:	Yes.
Jorge:	No. But I like that tracksuit.
Elena:	Which one? The black one? It's a little bit tacky, isn't it?
Jorge:	No. Black's very fashionable.
Elena:	And those shoes. Do you like them?
Jorge:	No, but I like those boots.
Elena:	Which ones? Those ones? They're really ugly.
Jorge:	No. They're fantastic.
Elena:	Jorge, you're really tacky!

Exercise 4.15

A recording of the completed conversation is available on the CD.

CD 2, track 8

Answers to exercise (in bold):

Elena:	¿Te gusta **aquella** camisa?
Jorge:	¿**Cuál**? ¿La verde?
Elena:	Sí.
Jorge:	No. Pero me gusta **aquel** chándal.
Elena:	¿**Cuál**? ¿El negro? Es un **poco** hortera, ¿no?
Jorge:	No. El negro está muy de **moda**
Elena:	Y **aquellos** zapatos. ¿Te gustan?
Jorge:	No, pero me gustan **aquellas** botas.
Elena:	¿**Cuáles**? ¿Ésas? Son muy feas.
Jorge:	No. Son **fantásticas**
Elena:	Jorge, ¡qué hortera **eres**!

Exercise 4.16
CD 2, track 9

Paco:	¿Qué pantalón te gusta? ¿Éste, ése o aquél?
Julio:	Me gusta ése. ¿Qué camisa te gusta?
Paco:	Me gusta aquélla.
Julio:	¿No prefieres ésta?
Paco:	No, prefiero aquélla.

Translation:

Paco:	Which pair of trousers do you like? This one, that one, or that one over there?
Julio:	I like that one. Which shirt do you like?
Paco:	I like that one over there.
Julio:	Don't you prefer this one?
Paco:	No, I prefer that one over there.

Exercise 4.17

Answer to exercise:

Paco:	¿Qué **zapatos** te **gustan**? ¿**Éstos, ésos** o **aquéllos**?
Julio:	Me **gustan ésos**. ¿Qué **camisetas** te **gustan**?
Paco:	Me **gustan aquéllas**.
Julio:	¿No prefieres **éstas**?
Paco:	No, prefiero **aquéllas**.

Exercise 4.18
CD 2, track 10

Transcript:

Jorge:	¿Qué falda te gusta? ¿Ésta o aquélla?
Elena:	Me gusta ésta, la verde.
Jorge:	¿Por qué?
Elena:	Porque no es tan corta como aquélla.
Jorge:	Pero a mí me gustan las minifaldas.
Elena:	Estás mucho más guapo en pantalones.
Jorge:	Ja, ja...muy graciosa.
Dependienta:	Hola. ¿Os interesa algo?
Elena:	Sí. Me gustaría probarme esta falda.
Dependienta:	¿Qué talla tienes?
Elena:	La 38.
Dependienta:	Lo siento mucho. No quedan.
Elena:	¿No quedan?
Dependienta:	Es que están muy de moda. Se han vendido todas. ¿Y ésta, la minifalda, te gusta?
Elena:	A mí, no mucho, pero a mi novio, sí.
Dependienta:	Seguro que te sienta bien. Tienes muy buen tipo.
Elena:	Gracias, pero no sé….
Dependienta:	También te puedo hacer un descuento del 10 por ciento.
Elena:	Es que no estoy segura. ¿Y este pantalón? ¿Qué vale?
Dependienta:	¿Éste? 45 euros.
Elena:	¿Lo tienes de mi talla?
Dependienta:	A ver…..sí, aquí hay uno. ¿Quieres probártelo?

Elena:	*No hace falta. Hay muchísima gente y seguro que me sienta bien. Me lo quedo.*
Dependienta:	*¿Cómo vas a pagar, con tarjeta o en efectivo?*
Elena:	*Con tarjeta.*
Dependienta:	*Me das tu carné de identidad, por favor.*
Elena:	*Sí, un momento……. a ver……..me parece que está en el otro bolso.*
Dependienta:	*Lo siento. Sin el carné no puedo hacerlo.*
Elena:	*Entiendo. No pasa nada; vivo muy cerca. Vuelvo en seguida.*

Translation:

Jorge:	Which skirt do you like? This one or that one over there?
Elena:	I like this one, the green one.
Jorge:	Why?
Elena:	Because it's not as short as that one over there.
Jorge:	But I like miniskirts.
Elena:	You look a lot better in trousers.
Jorge:	Ha, ha… very funny.
Dependienta:	Hello. Is there something you like?
Elena:	Yes, I'd like to try this skirt on.
Dependienta:	What size are you?
Elena:	38.
Dependienta:	I'm really sorry. We haven't got any left.
Elena:	There aren't any left?
Dependienta:	The thing is they're really in fashion. We've sold all of them. And what about this one, the miniskirt, do you like it?
Elena:	Me, not much, but my boyfriend does.
Dependienta:	I'm sure it will really suit you. You've got a really nice figure.
Elena:	Thanks, but I don't know…
Dependienta:	I can also give you a discount of 10%.
Elena:	I'm not sure. And this pair of trousers? How much is it?
Dependienta:	This one? 45 euros.
Elena:	Have you got it in my size?
Dependienta:	Let's see….yes, here's one. Do you want to try them on?
Elena:	There's no need. It's really crowded and I'm sure they're the right size. I'll take them.
Dependienta:	How would you like to pay? Card or cash?
Elena:	By card.
Dependienta:	Can I have your identity card please?
Elena:	Yes, just a moment…… let's see…….I think it's in my other bag.
Dependienta:	I'm sorry. Without the card, I can't do it.
Elena:	I understand. No problem; I live really nearby. I'll be right back.

Answers to questions:
1. *Porque no es tan corta como la otra.*
2. *La 38.*
3. *Porque no quedan.*
4. *Dice que le sienta bien, que tiene muy buen tipo y que le va a hacer un descuento del 10 por ciento.*
5. *Porque hay mucha gente y piensa que le va a sentar bien.*
6. *Porque no tiene su carné de identidad.*

Translations:
1. Because it's not as short as the other one.
2. 38.
3. There are none left.
4. She says it suits her, that she has a really good figure and that she's going to give her a 10% discount.
5. Because it's crowded and she thinks it will fit.
6. Because she doesn't have her ID card.

Exercise 4.19

Suggestions: Conversations should be enacted and used for comprehension purposes.

Exercise 4.20

A recording of the conversation is available on the CD.

CD 2, track 11

Angela:	¿Qué te vas a poner para ir al instituto?
Elena:	No sé, algo cómodo.
Angela:	¿No tienes que llevar uniforme?
Elena:	No, claro que no.
Angela:	¡Qué suerte!
Elena:	¿Estás diciendo que tú tienes que ponerte uniforme?
Angela:	Sí. Tengo que ponerme una falda, unas medias, una chaqueta, e incluso una corbata.
Elena:	¿Y los chicos, también?
Angela:	Sí, claro. Bueno, ellos llevan pantalones en lugar de falda, y calcetines en vez de medias.
Elena:	Normal. Y los profesores, ¿qué ropa llevan?
Angela:	Depende. Los hombres suelen vestir un traje y una corbata, las mujeres una falda o un pantalón y una blusa. ¿Y aquí?
Elena:	Es más informal. Hay algunos profesores que llevan traje, pero muy pocos.
Angela:	Bueno, creo que me voy a poner un pantalón en lugar de una falda.
Elena:	Igual que yo. Dice el pronóstico del tiempo que va a hacer frío.

Translation:

Angela:	What are you going to wear to school?
Elena:	I don't know. Something confortable.
Angela:	Don't you have to wear a uniform?
Elena:	No, of course not.
Angela:	You're so lucky!
Elena:	Are you saying that you have to wear a uniform?
Angela:	Yes. I have to wear a skirt, stockings, a jacket and even a tie.
Elena:	And the boys too?
Angela:	Yes, of course. Well, they wear trousers instead of a skirt and socks instead of stockings.
Elena:	Nothing new there. And the teachers, what clothes do they wear?
Angela:	It depends. The men usually wear a suit and tie, the women a skirt or trousers, and a blouse. And here?
Elena:	It's more informal. There are some teachers who wear a suit, but very few.
Angela:	Well, I think I'm going to put on a pair of trousers instead of a skirt.
Elena:	Me too. The weather forecast says it's going to be cold.

Answers to questions:
1. *Porque no tiene que llevar uniforme.*
2. *Los chicos llevan pantalones en lugar de falda, y calcetines, en vez de medias.*
3. *Porque el pronóstico dice que va a hacer frío.*

Translations:
1. Because she doesn't have to wear a uniform.
2. The boys wear trousers instead of a skirt and socks rather than stockings.
3. Because the forecast says it's going to be cold.

Exercise 4.21
CD 2, track 12

Transcript:

Jorge:	¿Qué tal estoy, Pedro? Guapísimo, ¿verdad?
Pedro:	¿Sí, pero no irás a la discoteca vestido así, verdad?
Jorge:	¿Por qué no? ¿Qué problema hay?
Pedro:	La gente no va a la discoteca en chándal. Además, no te van a dejar entrar así.
Jorge:	¿Por qué no?
Pedro:	Porque es un sitio muy de moda y tú pareces un hortera así.
Jorge:	Pero este chándal está muy de moda.
Pedro:	Tienes que ponerte otra cosa.
Jorge:	¿Qué vas a ponerte tú?
Pedro:	Me voy a poner unos vaqueros, una camiseta roja de "Zara" y unas botas negras.
Jorge:	¿Tienes unos vaqueros para prestarme?
Pedro:	Sí, pero el problema es que no tenemos la misma talla.
Jorge:	Entonces, ¿qué hago?
Pedro:	Tienes que volver a casa y ponerte algo chulo.
Jorge:	No puedo.
Pedro:	¿Por qué?
Jorge:	Porque este chándal es la cosa más chula que tengo.
Pedro:	Es temprano todavía. Ve a "Zara" y compra algo chulo.
Jorge:	No puedo. No tengo dinero.
Pedro:	Toma, aquí tienes 80 euros.
Jorge:	Estás loco. ¿Me vas a dar 80 euros?
Pedro:	Te los presto. No hay problema.
Jorge:	Muchísimas gracias. ¿Vienes conmigo?
Pedro:	No puedo. Tengo un montón de deberes que hacer. Pero, pregunta por una dependienta que se llama Yolanda. Es muy amiga mía y tiene mucho estilo. Ella te puede dar unos buenos consejos.
Jorge:	Vale. ¿Y dónde quedamos luego?
Pedro:	¿Quedamos en el bar, al lado de la discoteca, a las 11?
Jorge:	De acuerdo. Hasta luego.

Translation:

Jorge:	How do I look, Pedro? Gorgeous, am I right?
Pedro:	Yes, but you're not going to the disco dressed like that, are you?
Jorge:	Why not? What's the problem?
Pedro:	People don't go to the disco in a tracksuit. Besides, they won't let you in like that.
Jorge:	Why not?
Pedro:	Because it's a really trendy place and you look like really tacky.

Jorge:	But this tracksuit's really trendy.
Pedro:	You have to put on something else.
Jorge:	What are you going to wear?
Pedro:	I'm going to wear some jeans, a red T-shirt from "Zara" and some black boots.
Jorge:	Could you lend me some jeans?
Pedro:	I've got some, but the problem is we're not the same size.
Jorge:	So, what do I do?
Pedro:	You have to go home and put something cool on.
Jorge:	I can't.
Pedro:	Why not?
Jorge:	Because this tracksuit is the coolest thing I've got.
Pedro:	It's still early. Go to "Zara" and buy something cool.
Jorge:	I can't. I haven't got any money.
Pedro:	Here you go, have 80 euros.
Jorge:	Are you crazy? You're giving me 80 euros?
Pedro:	I'm lending them to you. It's not a problem.
Jorge:	Thanks so much. Will you come with me?
Pedro:	I can't. I've got masses of homework to do. But ask for an assistant called Yolanda. She's a good friend of mine and is very trendy. She can give you some good advice.
Jorge:	OK. Where shall we meet later?
Pedro:	Shall we meet in the bar next to the disco at 11?
Jorge:	OK. See you later.

Answers to questions:
1. *Porque lleva un chándal y parece un hortera*
2. *Unos vaqueros, una camiseta roja de "Zara" y unas botas negras.*
3. *Porque no tienen la misma talla.*
4. *Para ponerse algo más chulo.*
5. *80 euros para comprar algo chulo.*
6. *Tiene muchos deberes que hacer.*
7. *Es una amiga de Pedro que tiene mucho estilo y que trabaja en "Zara".*
8. *En el bar, al lado de la discoteca a las 11.*

Translations:
1. Because he's wearing a tracksuit and looks tacky.
2. Jeans, a red T-shirt from "Zara" and some black boots.
3. They don't have the same size.
4. To go and put on something more trendy/cool.
5. 80 euros to buy something cool/trendy.
6. He's got lots of homework to do.
7. She's a friend of Pedro who is very trendy and who works in "Zara."
8. In the bar next to the disco at 11.

Exercise 4.22

A recording of the conversation is available on the CD.

UNIT 4 | 67

CD 2, track 13

Padre:	Bueno chicos, ¿cuándo os vais a cambiar de ropa? Tenemos la mesa reservada a las diez.
Paco:	¿Por qué no podemos ir así?
Padre:	Porque estáis en pantalones cortos.
Paco:	Pero estoy asado; hace muchísimo calor. Vamos a estar mucho más cómodos así.
Padre:	El restaurante tiene aire acondicionado.
Julio:	¿Es que no vamos a comer fuera?
Padre:	Creo que vamos a estar mejor dentro. Hace mucho calor para estar fuera.
Julio:	Pero hay un jardín enorme fuera y podemos jugar al fútbol.
Padre:	No vamos al restaurante para jugar al fútbol. Vamos a comer.
Julio:	Pero Papá, mañana tenemos un partido muy importante y queremos practicar.
Padre:	Lo siento. No puede ser.
Madre:	Anda, Jesús, déjalos.
Padre:	Que no. Y, como he dicho antes, tenéis que cambiaros de ropa.
Paco:	¿Qué me tengo que poner?
Padre:	Un pantalón, para empezar.
Paco:	¿Mis vaqueros?
Padre:	No. Siempre están sucios. Y ponte una camisa limpia y planchada.
Paco:	¿Puedo llevar las zapatillas?
Padre:	No, no pegan con el pantalón y la camisa. Pónte esos zapatos de cuero que tienes.
Julio:	¿Y yo? ¿Qué me pongo?
Padre:	Lo mismo que tu hermano.
Madre:	¿T tú, Jesús, qué te vas a poner?
Padre:	Mi traje nuevo. El dueño del restaurante es un cliente del banco y quiero causar una buena impresión. ¿Y tú?
Madre:	Yo me voy a poner ese vestido blanco. Así voy fresquita.

Translation:

Padre:	Well, boys, when are you going to change? The table's booked for 10.
Paco:	Why can't we go like this?
Padre:	Because you're in shorts.
Paco:	But I'm boiling; it's really hot. We're going to be much more comfortable like this.
Padre:	The restaurant's got air-conditioning.
Julio:	Aren't we going to eat outside?
Padre:	I think we're going to be better off inside. It's very hot to be outside.
Julio:	But there's an enormous garden outside and we can play football.
Padre:	We're not going to the restaurant to play football. We're going there to eat.
Julio:	But Dad, we've got a really important football match tomorrow and we want to practise.
Padre:	I'm sorry. It can't be.
Madre:	Oh go on, Jesús, let them.
Padre:	No. And as I said before, you've got to get changed.
Paco:	What do I have to put on?
Padre:	A pair of trousers to start with.
Paco:	My jeans?
Padre:	No. They're always dirty. And put on a clean, ironed shirt.
Paco:	Can I wear my trainers?
Padre:	No, they don't go with the trousers and shirt. Put on those leather shoes you've got.

Julio:	And me? What should I wear?
Padre:	The same as your brother.
Madre:	And you Jesús, what are you going to put on?
Padre:	My new suit. The owner of the restaurant is a client of the bank and I want to make a good impression. And you?
Madre:	I'm going to put on that white dress. That way I'll go nice and cool.

Answers to questions:
1. *Porque están en pantalones cortos y van a comer en un restaurante.*
2. *Porque hace mucho calor y el restaurante tiene aire acondicionado.*
3. *Quieren jugar al fútbol, porque tienen un partido muy importante mañana.*
4. *Porque siempre están muy sucios.*
5. *Porque no pegan con el pantalón y la camisa.*
6. *La misma que su hermano.*
7. *Un traje nuevo, puesto que quiere causar una buena impresión.*
8. *Su vestido blanco porque así va fresquita.*
9. *En un banco.*

Translations:
1. Because they're wearing shorts and they're going to have a meal in a restaurant.
2. Because it's very hot and the restaurant has air-conditioning.
3. They want to play football as they have a very important match tomorrow.
4. Because they're always really dirty.
5. Because they don't go with the trousers and shirt.
6. The same as his brother.
7. A new suit as he wants to make a good impression.
8. Her white dress as she'll be fresh/cool like that.
9. In a bank.

Exercise 4.23

Suggestions: This exercise should be used for additional comprehension work. Pupils could be asked questions such as:
¿Adónde va el hijo/la hija?
¿Qué quiere llevar?
¿Por qué no puede ir vestido/a así?
¿Qué ropa tiene que ponerse?

Unit 5

About the unit
In this unit pupils will learn to use a range of tenses to talk and write about trips and holidays.

New language content:
- preterite tense of the irregular verb *ir*
- preterite tense or regular *–ar* verbs

New contexts:
- holidays and tourism
- outings and trips
- modes of transport

Expectations
At the end of this unit most pupils will be able to: understand information about transport, outings and holidays; take part in conversations about plans for the weekend and holidays; describe a holiday or an outing in the preterite tense (using *ir* and regular *–ar* verbs), detailing where you went, how you travelled, and, to some extent, what you did; read and comprehend texts about holidays, deducing meanings and using a dictionary where necessary.

This unit should begin with revision of the words that were learnt in Unit 5 in Book one, *En el pueblo*. This could be done either by asking pupils to recite words from memory, or by asking specific questions, e.g. *¿Cómo se dice* baker's *en español?*

Exercise 5.1
CD 2, track 14

Transcript:

Pedro:	*Hola, Elena, ¿qué tal?*
Elena:	*Muy bien. ¿Y tú?*
Pedro:	*Bien. ¿Adónde vas?*
Elena:	*A Correos. Tengo que mandar una carta a Inglaterra.*
Pedro:	*¿Por qué?*
Elena:	*Voy a Londres este verano. Voy a quedarme con mi amiga inglesa Ángela. Tengo que darle los detalles de mi viaje.*
Pedro:	*¿Cuándo te vas?*
Elena:	*En julio. Ángela dice que hace mejor tiempo. Y tú, ¿adónde vas?*
Pedro:	*Voy a la agencia de viajes.*
Elena:	*¿Para qué?*
Pedro:	*Me gustaría ir a Italia. Quiero ir en junio porque no hace tanto calor como en julio y agosto.*
Elena:	*¿Por qué Italia?*
Pedro:	*Me encantan el idioma y la gente. La comida tampoco está mal.*
Elena:	*Hablando de la comida, ¿tienes prisa?*
Pedro:	*No, ¿por qué?*
Elena:	*¿Vamos a la cafetería para merendar?*
Pedro:	*Sí, vale.*

Translation:

Pedro:	Hi, Elena, how are you?
Elena:	Really well. And you?
Pedro:	Good. Where are you going?
Elena:	To the Post Office. I have to send a letter to England.
Pedro:	Why?
Elena:	I'm going to London this summer. I'm going to stay with my English friend Angela. I have to give her the details of my trip.
Pedro:	When are you going?
Elena:	In July. Angela says the weather's better then. And you, where are you going?
Pedro:	I'm going to the travel agents.
Elena:	What for?
Pedro:	I'd like to go to Italy. I want to go in June as it's not as hot as in July and August.
Elena:	Why Italy?
Pedro:	I love the language and the people. The food's not bad either.
Elena:	Talking about food, are you in a hurry?
Pedro:	No. Why?
Elena:	Shall we go to the cafeteria for tea?
Pedro:	Yes, OK.

Answers to questions:
1. *Va a Correos porque tiene que mandar una carta a Londres.*
2. *Inglaterra, para quedarse con su amiga inglesa.*
3. *En julio, porque hace mejor tiempo.*
4. *A la agencia de viajes, porque le gustaría ir a Italia.*
5. *Italia, porque le gustan el idioma, la gente y la comida.*
6. *En junio, puesto que no hace tanto calor como en julio y agosto.*
7. *A la cafetería, para merendar.*

UNIT 5 | 71

Translations:
1. She's going to the Post Office as she has to send a letter to London.
2. England, to stay with an English friend.
3. In July, because the weather's better.
4. To the travel agents, as he wants to go to Italy.
5. Italy, as he likes the language, the people and the food.
6. In June, because it's not as hot as in July and August.
7. To the cafeteria, to have tea.

Exercise 5.2

Pupils should be asked to enact their dialogues, and questions asked accordingly, e.g. *¿Adónde va X, y por qué? ¿Adónde va Y, y por qué?*

Exercise 5.3

A recording of the conversation is available on the CD.

CD 2, track 15

Carmen: *Entonces, ¿qué planes tienes para el verano?*
Rosa: *Todavía no estoy segura. Depende de mi trabajo en la tienda. Si tengo dinero suficiente me gustaría ir al extranjero, pero si no, supongo que iré a la playa con mis padres. ¿Y tú?*
Carmen: *Bueno, mi amiga inglesa Poppy me ha invitado a su casa en Londres, pero ya conozco Inglaterra un poco y tengo ganas de ir a otro sitio.*
Rosa: *¿Dónde por ejemplo?*
Carmen: *No sé. Los Estados Unidos, Australia, La India, un país exótico así. El problema es que no me gusta mucho volar. Además, va a costar mucho. Entonces pienso que no va a ser posible.*
Rosa: *¿Y por qué no vas a un país más cercano como Francia o Italia?*
Carmen: *No hablo francés y me han dicho que eso puede ser un problema. Italia, la conozco ya. Una de las hermanas de mi madre está casada con un italiano y vive en Roma. He ido a verlos varias veces. Y tú, si tienes dinero, ¿adónde vas a ir?*
Rosa: *Me gustaría mucho conocer Irlanda. Yo no aguanto el calor, y creo que nunca hace calor en Irlanda. Además, me han dicho que la gente es muy simpática. También, la cerveza irlandesa me encanta, sobre todo la "Guinness".*

Translation:
Carmen: So, what plans have you got for the summer?
Rosa: I'm still not sure. It depends on my job in the shop. If I've got enough money, I'd like to go abroad, but if not, I suppose I'll go to the beach with my parents. And you?
Carmen: Well, my English friend Poppy has invited me to her house in London, but I already know England a little and I feel like going somewhere else.
Rosa: Like where?
Carmen: I don't know. The US, Australia, India, an exotic country like that. The problem is I don't like flying. Besides, it's going to be really expensive. So I don't think it's going to happen.
Rosa: And why don't you go somewhere nearer like France or Italy?
Carmen: I don't speak French and I've heard that can be a problem. And as for Italy, the thing is I already know it. One of my mother's sisters is married to an Italian and lives in Rome. I've been to see them a few times. And you, if you've got some money, where are you going to go?
Rosa: I'd really like to know Ireland. I can't stand the heat and I think it's never hot in Ireland. Besides, I've heard that the people are really nice. I also like Irish beer, especially Guinness.

Answers to questions:
1. *Porque no sabe el dinero que va a tener.*
2. *Porque ya conoce Inglaterra y tiene ganas de ir a otro sitio.*
3. *Puesto que no le gusta volar y va a ser muy caro.*
4. *No habla francés y ya conoce Italia porque tiene una tía que vive allí.*
5. *Porque está casada con un italiano.*
6. *A Irlanda, puesto que no hace calor, la gente es simpática, y le gusta la cerveza irlandesa.*

Translations:
1. Because she doesn't know how much money she's going to have.
2. Because she already knows England and wants to go somewhere new.
3. Because she doesn't like flying and it's going to be very expensive.
4. She doesn't speak French and she already knows Italy as she has an aunt who lives there.
5. As she is married to an Italian.
6. Ireland, as it's not hot, the people are kind, and she likes Irish beer.

Exercise 5.4

Suggestions: It would be worth revising names of individual countries before undertaking this exercise. As usual, dialogues should be enacted and used for comprehension work. Possible questions might include:

¿Adónde le gustaría ir a X y por qué no va a ser posible?
¿Adónde va a ir?
¿Por qué quiere ir allí?

Exercise 5.5
CD 2, track 16

Transcript:

Padre:	*Tenemos que hablar de las vacaciones. Como voy a comprar un coche nuevo para vuestra madre y una moto nueva para vosotros, solamente vamos a poder ir de vacaciones una vez este año. A mí me gustaría ir a Noruega o Finlandia en verano. Hay muchísima menos gente allí y hace mucho menos calor que en España. Allí podemos descansar, hacer vela, leer.*
Paco:	*Pero Papá, allí hace frío y nosotros nos aburrimos. ¿Por qué no vamos a Grecia? Allí también se puede hacer vela y todas las cosas que a ti te gustan. Y Julio y yo podemos ir a la playa, jugar al tenis, jugar al golf, tomar el sol, salir por las noches. Y si vamos en julio no va a haber tanta gente como en agosto.*
Julio:	*Yo prefiero quedarme aquí en España. ¿Por qué no volvemos a Almuñécar? Si vamos a casa de los abuelos no nos va a costar nada. Y es mejor ir en agosto. Todos nuestros amigos estarán allí, y los tuyos, también, Papá. Puedes jugar al dominó con tus amigos; Mamá puede tomar el sol y leer sus revistas, y nosotros podemos hacer esquí acuático, jugar al tenis, y salir en la barca.*
Paco:	*Pero siempre podemos ir a Almuñécar. Es mejor ir a un sitio nuevo.*
Madre:	*Yo estoy de acuerdo, pero ¿por qué no vamos de vacaciones en Navidad? Nunca vamos a ninguna parte en diciembre o enero. Podemos ir a Francia, Italia, Austria o Suiza. A mí me encantaría ir a esquiar.*
Padre:	*No tenemos que ir al extranjero para eso. Aquí hay muchas estaciones de esquí.*
Madre:	*Sí, pero hemos esquiado aquí muchas veces. Yo tengo ganas de ir a otro país.*
Julio:	*Sí, está bien. De todas formas, como el piso en Almuñécar es gratis, podemos veranear allí como siempre.*
Padre:	*Bueno, ya veremos.*

UNIT 5 | 73

Translation:

Padre: We have to speak about the holidays. As I'm going to buy your mother a new car and buy you a new scooter, we're only going to be able to have one holiday this year. I'd like to go to Norway or Finland this summer. There are far less people there and it's much less hot. There we can rest, go sailing, read.

Paco: But Dad, it's cold there and we get bored. Why don't we go to Greece? You can go sailing there and do all the other things you like. And Julio and I can go to the beach, play tennis, play golf, sunbathe, go out at night. And if we go in July, there won't be so many people as in August.

Julio: I prefer to stay here in Spain. Why don't we go back to Almuñécar? If we go to our grandparents' place it won't cost us anything. And it's better to go in August. All our friends will be there and yours too, Dad. You can play dominos with your friends, Mum can sunbathe and read her magazines and we can go waterskiing, play tennis and go out in the boat.

Paco: But we can always go to Almuñécar. It's better to go somewhere new.

Madre: I agree, but why don't we go on holiday at Christmas? We never go anywhere in December or January. We can go to France, Italy, Austria or Switzerland? I'd love to go skiing.

Padre: We don't have to go abroad for that. There are lots of ski resorts here.

Madre: Yes, but we've been skiing here lots of times. I feel like going to another country.

Julio: Yes, that's a good idea. Anyway, as the flat in Almuñécar is free, we can spend the summer holidays there like always.

Padre: Well, we'll see.

Answers to questions:

1. A Noruega o Finlandia, en el verano.
2. Porque hay muchísima menos gente allí y hace mucho menos calor que en España. Se puede descausar, hacer vela, leer.
3. A Grecia, en julio. Su padre puede hacer vela allí y las otras cosas que le gustan. También, Paco y Julio pueden ir a la playa, jugar al tenis y al golf, tomar el sol y salir por las noches.
4. Julio prefiere quedarse en España.
5. En agosto, puesto que todos sus amigos estarán/van a estar allí. También van a estar los amigos de su padre.
6. Quiere ir a un sitio nuevo.
7. Prefiere ir de vacaciones en Navidad ya que nunca van a ninguna parte en diciembre o enero.

Translations:

1. To Norway or Finland, in the summer.
2. Because there are far less people there and it's much less hot than in Spain. They can rest, go sailing, read.
3. To Greece, in July. His father can go sailing there and also do the other things he likes. Also, Paco and Julio can go to the beach, play tennis and golf, sunbathe and go out at night.
4. He prefers to stay in Spain.
5. In August because all his friends will be there. His father's friends will be there also.
6. He wants to go somewhere new.
7. She prefers to go on holiday at Christmas as they never go away in December or January.

Exercise 5.6

A recording of the conversation is available on the CD.

CD 2, track 17

Agente:	Buenos días.
Padre:	Buenos días.
Agente:	¿Cómo puedo ayudarle?
Padre:	Necesito infomación sobre estaciones de esquí.
Agente:	Vale. ¿En este país o en el extranjero?
Padre:	En el extranjero.
Agente:	¿Qué países le interesan?
Padre:	Los más baratos.
Agente:	¿Cuándo quiere ir?
Padre:	En Navidad. Después de Nochebuena. No podemos ir antes porque vienen mis suegros a quedarse con nosotros. No se van hasta el 28 de diciembre.
Agente:	¿Cuántas personas?
Padre:	Cuatro. Mi mujer y yo y nuestros dos hijos.
Agente:	¿Qué edad tienen?
Padre:	Dieciséis y dieciocho años.
Agente:	¿Cuánto tiempo quieren estar?
Padre:	No estoy seguro; depende del precio.

Translation:

Agente:	Good morning.
Padre:	Good morning.
Agente:	How can I help you?
Padre:	I need some information about ski resorts.
Agente:	OK. In this country or abroad?
Padre:	Abroad.
Agente:	What countries are you interested in?
Padre:	The cheapest.
Agente:	When do you want to go?
Padre:	At Christmas. After Christmas Eve. We can't go before as my in-laws are coming to stay with us. They don't leave until December 28th.
Agente:	How many people?
Padre:	Four. My wife, me and our two sons.
Agente:	How old are they?
Padre:	Sixteen and eighteen.
Agente:	How long do you want to go for?
Padre:	I'm not sure; it depends on the price.

Answers to questions:
1. Necesita información sobre estaciones de esquí.
2. Porque vienen los suegros a quedarse.
3. Porque depende del precio.

Translations:
1. He needs information about ski resorts.
2. The in-laws are coming to stay and don't leave until December 28th.
3. It depends on the price.

Exercise 5.7

Answers (in bold):

Agente:	Buenos días.
Padre:	Buenos días.
Agente:	¿**Cómo** puedo ayudarle?
Padre:	Necesito infomación sobre estaciones de esquí.
Agente:	Vale. ¿En este país o en el extranjero?
Padre:	En el extranjero.
Agente:	¿**Qué** países le interesan?
Padre:	Los más baratos.
Agente:	¿**Cuándo** quiere ir?
Padre:	En Navidad. Después de Nochebuena. No podemos ir antes porque vienen mis suegros a quedarse con nosotros. No se van hasta el 28 de diciembre.
Agente:	¿**Cuántas** personas?
Padre:	Cuatro. Mi mujer y yo y nuestros dos hijos.
Agente:	¿**Qué** edad tienen?
Padre:	Dieciséis y dieciocho.
Agente:	¿**Cuánto** tiempo quieren estar?
Padre:	No estoy seguro; depende del precio.

Exercise 5.8

Role plays could be enacted and used for oral work with questions from the teacher.

Exercise 5.9

Answers:

1. ¿Cómo quiere viajar?
2. ¿Cuándo quiere ir?
3. ¿Cuánto tiempo quiere estar?
4. ¿Qué países le gustan?
5. ¿Cuánto dinero puede gastar?

Exercise 5.10

As in Exercise 5.8, role plays could be enacted and used for oral work.

Exercise 5.11

Translation:

Dear Poppy

How are things? I'm very well, but a little nervous. It's my mother. She asks me a thousand questions each day about the trip. She's so annoying. I've now got my ticket. I leave on July 6th. I can't go before as I might have to redo some exams. I have to get the evening flight, that way my father can take me to Málaga in the Seat. I arrive at ten thirty. Can you meet me? I hope so as I don't know how to get to your house. Well, what are we going to do during the holidays? Are we going to go to Scotland? I hope so. I'd love to go back to the festival in Edinburgh. How long are we going to be there? What else are we going to do? And you, how are you? How's school? We're in the exam period here and so I've got a lot of work on. Well, I have to go. See if you can write back soon.

A big hug

Elena

Answers:
1. *Falsa. Elena está nerviosa a causa de su madre.*
2. *V.*
3. *Falsa. Va con su padre.*
4. *Falsa. Va a Málaga en coche.*
5. *V.*
6. *Falsa. Ya conoce Escocia.*
7. *V.*

Exercise 5.12
CD 2, track 18

Transcript:

Jorge:	*Tenemos que hablar del verano.*
Elena:	*Vale.*
Jorge:	*¿Qué vamos a hacer?*
Elena:	*Bueno, yo tengo un pequeño problema.*
Jorge:	*¿Cuál?*
Elena:	*Me voy a Inglaterra a ver a Poppy.*
Jorge:	*¿Qué dices?*
Elena:	*Pues eso, que me voy a Inglaterra.*
Jorge:	*No seas tonta. Tienes que estar conmigo.*
Elena:	*No me llames tonta, y puedo hacer lo que quiera.*
Jorge:	*Bueno, lo siento. Es que yo no sabía nada. Tengo una idea: Yo voy contigo.*
Elena:	*¡Ni hablar!*
Jorge:	*¿Por qué?*
Elena:	*Porque esto es un intercambio entre dos personas, no entre tres. Además, necesito tiempo para pensar en nuestro futuro.*
Jorge:	*¿Cómo?*
Elena:	*Lo que oyes.*
Jorge:	*¿Y cuánto tiempo vas a estar allí?*
Elena:	*En Londres dos semanas y luego, vamos a Escocia otras dos semanas.*
Jorge:	*¿Cómo vas?*
Elena:	*En avión.*
Jorge:	*Pero ir en avión no te gusta.*
Elena:	*Es mucho más rápido.*
Jorge:	*¿Y cuándo vuelves?*
Elena:	*La primera semana de agosto.*
Jorge:	*Entonces, podemos ir a alguna parte, juntos, en agosto.*
Elena:	*Ya veremos.*

Translation:

Jorge:	We have to speak about the summer.
Elena:	OK.
Jorge:	What are we going to do?
Elena:	Well, I've got a small problem.
Jorge:	Which one?
Elena:	I'm going to England to see Poppy.
Jorge:	What?
Elena:	Well just that, I'm going to England.
Jorge:	Don't be silly. You have to be with me.

Elena:	Don't call me silly, and I can do whatever I want.
Jorge:	OK, I'm sorry. It's just that I didn't know anything about this. I've got an idea: I'll go with you.
Elena:	No way.
Jorge:	Why not?
Elena:	Because this is an exchange between two people, not three. Besides, I need time to think about our future.
Jorge:	What?
Elena:	What you just heard.
Jorge:	And how long are you going to be there?
Elena:	2 weeks in London and then we're going to Scotland for 2 weeks.
Jorge:	How are you going?
Elena:	By 'plane.
Jorge:	But you don't like flying.
Elena:	It's a lot quicker.
Jorge:	And when are you coming back?
Elena:	The first week in August.
Jorge:	So, we can go somewhere together in August.
Elena:	We'll see.

Answers to questions:
1. *Se va a Inglaterra.*
2. *Quiere ir con Elena a Inglaterra.*
3. *Porque es un intercambio para dos personas. También, Elena necesita tiempo para pensar en su futuro.*
4. *Cuatro semanas/un mes.*
5. *Es mucho más rápido.*
6. *La primera semana de agosto.*

Translations:
1. She's going to England.
2. He wants to go with Elena to England.
3. Because it's an exchange trip between 2 people. Also, Elena needs time to think about their future.
4. 4 weeks/1 month.
5. It's a lot quicker.
6. The first week of August.

Exercise 5.13

Pupils should study (and translate) the brief conversation between Eva and Juan, which will act as a model for their work in the next exercise. A recording of the conversation is available on the CD.

CD 2, track 19

Eva:	*Hola Juan, ¿adónde vas?*
Juan:	*Hola. Voy a Almería, ¿y tú?*
Eva:	*Voy a Madrid. ¿Cómo vas?*
Juan:	*En autocar, ¿y tú?*
Eva:	*En tren.*
Juan:	*¡Que lo pases bien!*

Translation:
Eva: Hi Juan. Where are you going?
Juan: Hi. I'm going to Almería, and you?
Eva: I'm going to Madrid. How are you travelling?
Juan: By coach, and you?
Eva: By train.
Juan: Have a good time!

Exercise 5.14

Suggestions: Role-plays should be enacted and used for comprehension purposes. The conversation in Exercise 5.13 could serve as a model. Pupils may be interested to know that the name *A Coruña* is now widely used throughout Spain in stead of *La Coruña*.

Exercise 5.15

Answers (in bold):
1. Nosotros **vamos** a **comer** en el restaurante.
2. Mi madre **va** a **ir** a Madrid en coche.
3. ¿Tú **vas** a **ver** la película esta noche?
4. ¿Vosotros **vais** a **hacer** los deberes hoy o mañana?
5. Yo **voy** a **tomar** el sol en la playa.

Translations:
1. We're going to eat in the restaurant.
2. My mother's going to go to Madrid by car.
3. Are you going to watch the film this evening?
4. Are you going to do the homework today or tomorrow?
5. I'm going to sunbathe on the beach.

Exercise 5.16

Suggestions: Pupils should be asked to read out examples and others asked to translate orally into English.

Exercise 5.17

Answers to questions:
1. Fue a Francia el verano pasado.
2. Fuimos a las tiendas, ayer.
3. Fueron a Italia para esquiar.
4. Fui a la playa para tomar el sol.
5. ¿Fuiste a Grecia?
6. ¿Fuisteis a Escocia?

Exercise 5.18

Suggestions: Pupils should be asked to read out examples and these should be used for comprehension purposes. For homework, pupils could be asked to invent more sentences of their own.

Exercise 5.19
CD 2, track 20

Transcript:

Elena: Dime, Poppy, ¿dónde veraneas normalmente?
Poppy: ¿Qué es 'veranear', exactamente?
Elena: Significa pasar las vacaciones de verano. Yo, por ejemplo, suelo veranear en la costa, porque me encanta el mar y todas mis amigas están allí en agosto.
Poppy: Normalmente vamos al campo porque mis padres tienen una casa allí, pero no me gusta mucho porque es muy tranquilo y no tengo amigos allí. El año pasado no fuimos. Fuimos a Estados Unidos.
Elena: ¿Y eso?
Poppy: Mis abuelos viven allí. Mi abuela estaba enferma y fuimos a verla. ¿Adónde fuiste tú el año pasado?
Elena: Yo también fui a otro sitio. Fui a Asturias, en el norte de España. Tenemos familia allí. Es precioso, muy diferente al sur, todo muy verde, como aquí.
Poppy: ¿Te gustaría volver?
Elena: Sí, pero hay otros sitios que quiero conocer antes. Por ejemplo, quiero ir a Galicia y al País Vasco. Me dicen que hay unos sitios preciosos allí. ¿Y tú, dónde quieres ir en el futuro?
Poppy: Me encantaría ir a África. Quiero hacer un safari.

Translation:

Elena: Tell me, Poppy, where do you normally spend the summer holidays?
Poppy: What does the word 'veranear' mean exactly?
Elena: It means to spend the summer holidays. For example, I usually go to the coast because I love the sea and all my friends are there in August.
Poppy: We normally go to the country as my parents have a house there, but I don't like it as it's really quiet and I don't have any friends there. But last year we didn't go. We went to the United States.
Elena: How come?
Poppy: My grandparents live there. My granny was ill and we went to see her. Where did you go last year?
Elena: I went somewhere else too. I went to Asturias in the north of Spain. We've got family there. It's beautiful, very different from the south, everything's really green like here.
Poppy: Would you like to go back?
Elena: Yes, but there are other places I want to visit before. For example, I want to go to Galicia and the Basque Country. I'm told there are some beautiful places there. And you, where do you want to go in the future?
Poppy: I'd love to go to Africa. I want to go on a safari.

Answers to questions:
1. Significa pasar las vacaciones de verano.
2. En la costa, porque le gusta el mar y todas sus amigas están allí en agosto.
3. En el campo, puesto que sus padres tienen una casa allí.
4. Porque es muy tranquilo y no tiene amigos allí.
5. Fue a los Estados Unidos para ver a su abuela que vive allí.
6. Fue a Asturias. Le gustó mucho.
7. Elena quiere ir a Galicia y al País Vasco, y Poppy quiere ir a África.

Translations:
1. It means to spend the summer holidays.
2. At the coast as she likes the sea and all her friends are there in August.
3. In the country as her parents have a house there.
4. Because it's very quiet and she doesn't have any friends there.
5. She went to the U.S.A to se her grandmother who lives there.
6. She went to Asturias. She loved it.
7. Elena wants to go to Galicia and the Basque Country and Poppy wants to go to Africa.

Exercise 5.20

A recording of the conversation is available on the CD.

CD 2, track 21

Manolo:	Hola Jorge. ¿Qué tal? Fui a tu casa ayer, pero no estabas.
Jorge:	No, fui a la agencia de viajes.
Manolo:	¿Por qué?
Jorge:	Voy a ir a Escocia en julio para ver a Elena.
Manolo:	Qué bien, ¿no?
Jorge:	Espero que sí. Va a ser una sorpresa.
Manolo:	¿Fuiste al concierto por la noche?
Jorge:	No. Fui al supermercado. Vamos a hacer una barbacoa este fin de semana. Y tú, ¿fuiste al bar con esa chica?
Manolo:	Sí fuimos, pero estaba cerrado, así que fuimos a ver una película. Entonces, ¿vas a ir a Escocia? ¿Qué vas a hacer allí?
Jorge:	Pues primero, comprarme un paraguas. Dicen que llueve mucho allí.
Manolo:	Sí, pero eso está bien. Todo está muy verde; es precioso.
Jorge:	¿Lo conoces?
Manolo:	Sí. Fui con mi hermano hace dos años ¡Qué maravilla!

Translation:

Manolo:	Hi Jorge. How are you? I went to your house yesterday, but you weren't there.
Jorge:	No, I went to the travel agents.
Manolo:	Why?
Jorge:	I'm going to go to Scotland in July to see Elena.
Manolo:	That's great, isn't it?
Jorge:	I hope it will be. It's going to be a surprise.
Manolo:	Did you go to the concert in the evening?
Jorge:	No. I went to the supermarket. We're going to have a barbecue this weekend. And you, did you go to the bar with that girl?
Manolo:	Yes, we went, but it was closed, so we went to see a film. So, you're going to go to Scotland? What are you going to do there?
Jorge:	Well, first of all, buy an umbrella. I'm told it rains a lot there.
Manolo:	Yes, but that's good. Everything's really green; it's beautiful.
Jorge:	Do you know it?
Manolo:	Yes. I went with my brother two years ago. It was fantastic!

Answers to questions:
1. *Porque fue a la agencia de viajes.*
2. *Mentira – va a ser una sorpresa.*
3. *Fue al supermercado para comprar comida para la barbacoa.*
4. *Fue al cine con una chica.*
5. *Puesto que llueve mucho.*

Translations:
1. Because he went to the travel agents.
2. False – it's going to be a surprise.
3. He went to the supermarket to buy food for the barbecue.
4. He went to the cinema with a girl.
5. Because it rains a lot.

Exercise 5.21
CD 2, track 22

Transcript:

Nuria:	Hola chicos. Hace mucho que no os veo.
Carlos:	Es que yo fui a Mallorca la semana pasada con mis padres.
Nuria:	¿Y eso?
Carlos:	Mi abuelo vive allí y está muy enfermo.
Nuria:	Lo siento mucho.
Carlos:	Gracias. Creo que va a mejorar.
Nuria:	¿Tú fuiste con Carlos, Eva?
Eva:	No. Yo fui a Jerez con mi novio.
Nuria:	¿Para qué?
Eva:	Para ver el campeonato del mundo del motociclismo. Las motos me encantan. ¿Y tú? ¿Dónde fuiste?
Nuria:	Yo no fui a ninguna parte. Yo me quedé sola aquí.
Eva:	¿Por qué?
Nuria:	Mis padres están de vacaciones y yo tengo mucho trabajo. Tengo exámenes la semana que viene.
Eva:	¡Qué rollo!
Nuria:	Pues, sí.

Translation:

Nuria:	Hi, folks. Haven't seen you for a while.
Carlos:	Last week I went to Mallorca with my parents.
Nuria:	How come?
Carlos:	My grandad lives there and he's really ill.
Nuria:	I'm really sorry.
Carlos:	Thanks. I think he's going to get better.
Nuria:	Did you go with Carlos, Eva?
Eva:	No. I went to Jerez with my boyfriend.
Nuria:	What for?
Eva:	To see the World Motorcycling Championships. I love motorbikes. What about you?
Nuria:	I didn't go anywhere. I was on my own here.
Eva:	Why?
Nuria:	My parents are on holiday and I've got a lot of work. I've got exams next week.
Eva:	What a pain!
Nuria:	You could say that.

Suggested questions:
1. ¿Adónde fue Carlos, y por qué?
2. ¿Con quién fue?
3. ¿Adónde fue Eva, y por qué?
4. ¿Con quién fue?
5. ¿Adónde fue Nuria, y por qué?

Suggestions: Pupils should be instructed to reply in full sentences so that they become familiar with the use of *ir* in the preterite.

Suggested answers:
1. *Fue a Mallorca para ver a su abuelo.*
2. *Fue con sus padres.*
3. *Fue a Jerez para ver el campeonato del mundo de motociclismo.*
4. *Fue con su novio.*
5. *No fue a ninguna parte porque tiene mucho trabajo.*

Translations:
1. He went to Mallorca to see his grandfather.
2. He went with his parents.
3. She went to Jerez to watch the World Motorcycling Championships.
4. She went with her boyfriend.
5. She didn't go anywhere as she has a lot of work to do.

Exercise 5.22

Answers:

	COMPRAR	**VIAJAR**	**BAILAR**
Yo	*compré*	*viajé*	*bailé*
Tú	*compraste*	*viajaste*	*bailaste*
Él	*compró*	*viajó*	*bailó*
Nosotros	*compramos*	*viajamos*	*bailamos*
Vosotros	*comprasteis*	*viajasteis*	*bailasteis*
Ellos	*compraron*	*viajaron*	*bailaron*

Exercise 5.23

Answers:
1. *Viajamos a España en avión.*
2. *Compró un coche nuevo, ayer.*
3. *¿Qué compraste en las tiendas?*
4. *Anoche bailaron con dos chicas guapas/guapísimas.*
5. *Viajó a Escocia para ver a su novia.*
6. *Bailé hasta las dos.*
7. *¿Viajaste en tren?*
8. *¿Bailasteis con esas mujeres?*
9. *Compraron mucha carne.*
10. *Viajé a España en barco*

Suggestions: Either for homework or as an additional classroom task, pupils should be asked to invent sentences of their own.

Exercise 5.24
CD 2, track 23

Transcript:

Carlos:	*Eva, ¿adónde fuiste durante las vacaciones?*
Eva:	*Fui a la playa con mi novio. Fuimos en moto.*
Carlos:	*¿Qué tal lo pasaste?*
Eva:	*Fenomenal. Tomé el sol. Me bañé mucho. Y tú, ¿qué tal?*
Carlos:	*Fatal. Fui al campo con mis padres. Fuimos en bicicleta. ¡Qué horror! Lo pasé muy mal. No había nada que hacer. Jugué a las cartas con mi hermana, nada más.*
Eva:	*¡Qué rollo! Y tú, Nuria, ¿adónde fuiste?*

Nuria:	*Fui a las montañas. El coche de mi padre estaba estropeado, así que fuimos en tren.*
Eva:	*¿Qué tal?*
Nuria:	*Ni bien ni mal. A veces lo pasé bien, a veces no. Me gustó mucho montar a caballo.*

Translation:

Carlos:	Eva, where did you go in the holidays?
Eva:	I went to the beach with my boyfriend. We went by motorbike.
Carlos:	How was it?
Eva:	Fantastic. I sunbathed. I went swimming a lot. And how about you?
Carlos:	Terrible. I went to the country with my parents. We went by bike. What a nightmare! I had an awful time. There was nothing to do. I played cards with my sister, nothing else.
Eva:	What a pain! And you Nuria, where did you go?
Nuria:	I went to the mountains. My dad's car was broken, so we went by train.
Eva:	How was it?
Nuria:	Neither good nor bad. Sometimes I had a good time, sometimes I didn't. I really enjoyed horseriding.

Suggestions: The following questions should be asked for each person:
1. *¿Adónde fue?*
2. *¿Cómo fue?*
3. *¿Qué tal lo pasó?*
4. *¿Qué hizo?*

N.B. The meaning of *hizo* may need to be explained.

Answers for Eva:
Fue a la playa. Fue en moto. Lo pasó muy bien/fenomenal. Tomó el sol y se bañó.

Answers for Carlos:
Fue al campo. Fue en bicicleta. Lo pasó fatal. Jugó a las cartas.

Answers for Nuria:
Fue a las montañas. Fue en tren. Lo pasó regular. Montó a caballo.

Exercise 5.25

Suggestions: Before pupils read out their dialogues, the others should be instructed to take notes. They will then be prepared to answer teacher-led questions afterwards. They should be reminded that, when answering questions, they will need to answer in the 3rd person.

Exercise 5.26

Answers (in bold):

Hola Ángela:

Ya estoy otra vez en España. Hace un mes **fui** *a Londres para ver a mi amiga Poppy. Lo* **pasé** *muy bien. Poppy me* **llevó** *a muchos sitios, sobre todo, a tiendas.* **Compré** *mucha ropa chula. La segunda semana, Poppy y yo* **fuimos** *a Escocia. Yo* **intenté** *hablar con la gente pero era muy difícil. ¿Qué tal tus vacaciones? ¿***Fuiste** *a la playa? Mándame noticias.*

Un beso,

Elena

Translation:

Hi Angela

Here I am back in Spain. A month ago I went to London to see my friend Poppy. I had a great time. Poppy took me to lots of places, especially shops. I bought lots of really cool clothes. In the second week we went to Scotland. I tried to speak to the people there, but it was really difficult. How were your holidays? Did you go to the beach? Send me your news.

A big kiss

Elena

Exercise 5.27

Pupils could be asked to read out their replies, and questions could be asked about the content.

Exercise 5.28

Answers:

Levantarse:

Yo **me levanté**	nosotros **nos levantamos**
Tú **te levantaste**	vosotros **os levantasteis**
Él **se levantó**	ellos **se levantaron**

Bañarse:

Yo **me bañé**	nosotros **nos bañamos**
Tú **te bañaste**	vosotros **os bañasteis**
Él **se bañó**	ellos **se bañaron**

Exercise 5.29

Suggestions: Pupils should be encouraged to read out their stories whilst the others take notes in order to answer teacher-led questions afterwards. If there are sufficient dictionaries in the class then pupils can be told to use them. Alternatively, it is worth asking them to use words that they already know.

Exercise 5.30

CD2: 24

A recording of the conversation is available on the CD.

CD 2, track 24

Answers (in bold):

Manolo:	Hola Jorge. ¿Qué tal lo **pasaste** en Escocia?
Jorge:	Regular. Elena estaba enfadadísima. No me **habló**.
Manolo:	¿Qué?
Jorge:	Bueno, me **habló**, pero solamente para llamarme gordo, asqueroso y feo.
Manolo:	¡Qué injusto! No eres ni asqueroso ni feo.
Jorge:	¡Qué gracioso!
Manolo:	Lo siento. ¿**Te quedaste** con ella y su amiga?
Jorge:	No. No me **dejaron**. **Me quedé** en un parque, en un banco.
Manolo:	¿Con o sin jacuzzi?
Jorge:	¡Muy divertido! Y tú, ¿qué tal?
Manolo:	**Fui** a la playa. **Me quedé** con mi abuela.
Jorge:	¿Qué tal lo pasaste?
Manolo:	**Lo pasé** mejor que tú, seguro.

Exercise 5.31

Answer (and translation to above):

Manolo:	Hi Jorge. How did you get on in Scotland?
Jorge:	Not so good. Elena was furious. She didn't speak to me.
Manolo:	What?
Jorge:	Well, she did speak to me, but only to call me disgusting, fat and ugly.
Manolo:	That's so unfair. You're not disgusting or ugly.
Jorge:	Very funny.
Manolo:	I'm sorry. Did you stay with her and her friend?
Jorge:	No. They didn't let me. I stayed in a park, on a bench.
Manolo:	With or without a jacuzzi?
Jorge:	Very funny. And what about you?
Manolo:	I went to the beach. I stayed with my grandmother.
Jorge:	What sort of time did you have?
Manolo:	I had a better time than you, that's for sure.

Unit 6

About the unit

In this unit pupils will learn to talk and write about a variety of events in the past. They will consolidate their knowledge of the preterite tense.

New language content:

- all forms of the preterite tense of regular *–er* and *–ir* verbs, e.g. *comer, salir* and irregular verbs such as *hacer, ver, estar*
- certain uses of the imperfect tense

New contexts:

- entertainment
- concerts, cinema, theatre, sport, a bullfight
- ordering and buying tickets
- describing a past event or an outing

Expectations

At the end of this unit most pupils will be able to: buy tickets for a range of different entertainments, offer alternatives and make arrangements; make plans with friends to go to an event; describe an outing in the past tense, including details about where you went, with whom, and how you got there. You may also be able to include extra details about times and descriptions of people and places.

Exercise 6.1

A recording of the conversation is available on the CD.

CD 2, track 25

Manolo:	Dígame.
Jorge:	Hola. Soy Jorge.
Manolo:	Hola Jorge. ¿Qué tal?
Jorge:	Fatal. Después de todo este tiempo, Elena todavía no me habla. La llamo todos los días pero su madre dice que no quiere hablar conmigo. Estoy hecho polvo. ¿Podemos hacer algo juntos?
Manolo:	Claro, hombre. ¿Qué te apetece?
Jorge:	No sé, cualquier cosa.
Manolo:	¿Te apetece ir al cine, por ejemplo?
Jorge:	No mucho. Fui ayer con mis padres.
Manolo:	¿Quieres ir al concierto de "Ketama"?
Jorge:	Me encantaría. Los vi hace dos años y fue fantástico. ¿Cuándo es?
Manolo:	Mañana.
Jorge:	Pero va a ser imposible conseguir entradas.
Manolo:	No te preocupes. Tengo enchufe. Tengo un amigo que conoce al grupo muy bien. Él me puede conseguir entradas, seguro.
Jorge:	Pues sí, tío. Sería un punto. ¿Dónde quedamos?
Manolo:	No sé. Tocan en la plaza de toros. Podemos quedar allí o, como yo voy en moto, te puedo recoger y podemos ir juntos.
Jorge:	Vale. Estupendo.
Manolo:	Te veo en tu casa a eso de las nueve. Si hay algún problema te llamo, ¿vale?
Jorge:	Vale. Hasta luego, y muchas gracias.
Manolo:	De nada, hombre. Hasta mañana.

Translation:

Manolo:	Hello.
Jorge:	Hi, it's Jorge.
Manolo:	Hi Jorge, how's it going?
Jorge:	Terrible. Alter all this time, Elena's still not talking to me. I call every day, but her mother says she doesn't want to speak to me. I'm distraught. Can we get together and do something?
Manolo:	Of course, mate. What do you feel like doing?
Jorge:	I don't know. Anything.
Manolo:	Do you feel like going to the cinema for example?
Jorge:	Not much. I went yesterday with my parents.
Manolo:	Do you want to go to the Ketama concert?
Jorge:	I'd love to. I saw them 2 years ago and it was fantastic. When is it?
Manolo:	Tomorrow.
Jorge:	But it's going to be impossible to get tickets.
Manolo:	Don't worry. I've got contacts. I've got a friend who knows the band really well. He can get tickets, no problem.
Jorge:	Well then that would be great man. Where shall we meet?
Manolo:	I don't know. They're performing at the bullring. We can meet there or, as I'm going by moped, I can pick you up and we can go together.
Jorge:	OK. Great.
Manolo:	I'll see you at your house at around nine. If there's any problem, I'll call you, OK?
Jorge:	OK. See you, and thanks a lot.
Manolo:	No problem. See you tomorrow.

Answers to questions:
1. Because Elena is still not talking to him.
2. He went yesterday with his parents.
3. He saw the group 2 years ago and it was fantastic.
4. He has a friend who knows the band really well.
5. At the bullring.
6. On Manolo's moped/motorbike.

Exercise 6.2

A recording of the conversation is available on the CD.

CD 2, track 26

Answer (suggested translation of dialogue):

Carlos:	¿Te apetece salir esta noche?
Ana:	Me encantaría. ¿Adónde quieres ir?
Carlos:	¿Vamos al cine?
Ana:	¿Qué ponen?
Carlos:	La nueva película de Almodóvar.
Ana:	Fantástico. ¿A qué hora empieza?
Carlos:	Hay una sesión a las ocho y media.
Ana:	Vale. ¿Dónde quedamos y a qué hora?
Carlos:	A las ocho y cuarto, en la taquilla.
Ana:	Vale. Hasta luego.
Carlos:	Hasta luego.

Exercise 6.3

Suggestions: Before getting pupils to invent dialogues, it is important to revise/ go over key vocabulary such as *el concierto, el estadio, el teatro, la plaza de toros, el circo, el palacio de deportes, el polideportivo*. Dialogues should be read out and used for comprehension purposes as usual.

Exercise 6.4

Answers (in bold):

Yo	**volví**	**salí**
Tú	**volviste**	**saliste**
Él	**volvió**	**salió**
Nosotros	**volvimos**	**salimos**
Vosotros	**volvisteis**	**salisteis**
Ellos	**volvieron**	**salieron**

Exercise 6.5

Answers:
1. *Comí muchas gambas ayer.*
2. *Volvió a España sin su novia.*
3. *'¿Cuándo volviste?' preguntó su madre.*
4. *Salimos después de cenar.*
5. *Salí con una chica guapísima anoche.*

Suggestions: Either as homework or additional classwork, pupils can be asked to create some more sentences of their own invention.

Exercise 6.6
CD 2, track 27

Transcript:

Carlos:	Hola Nuria. ¿Te apetece salir esta noche?
Nuria:	No sé. Es que tengo exámenes pasado mañana y tengo mucho trabajo.
Carlos:	Sí, pero también tienes que descansar.
Nuria:	¿Adónde quieres ir?
Carlos:	¿Tienes ganas de ver las procesiones?
Nuria:	Me gustaría, pero va a haber muchísima gente, ¿no?
Carlos:	Sí, pero no pasa nada. Es más emocionante con más gente.
Nuria:	Bueno, vale. ¿Dónde quedamos?
Carlos:	¿Qué tal si nos vemos en el bar del hotel "Reina Cristina"? Es muy céntrico y, además, ponen unas tapas riquísimas.
Nuria:	Lo que pasa es que tengo la moto estropeada y está en el taller.
Carlos:	¿No puedes ir en autobús? El 8 pasa por la puerta.
Nuria:	No. Siempre hay que esperar mucho. Mi padre me llevará en coche. ¿A qué hora nos vemos?
Carlos:	Tengo un partido de fútbol hasta las ocho. Luego, me tengo que duchar. ¿Qué tal si quedamos en el bar a las nueve y media?
Nuria:	Vale. Te veo luego.
Carlos:	Muy bien. Hasta luego.

Translation:

Carlos:	Hi Nuria. Do you feel like going out tonight?
Nuria:	I don't know. The thing is I've got exams the day after tomorrow and I've got a lot of work.
Carlos:	Yes, but you also have to rest.
Nuria:	Where do you want to go?
Carlos:	Do you feel like going to see the processions?
Nuria:	I'd like to, but there are going to be an awful lot of people, won't there?
Carlos:	Yes, but that's all right. It's more exciting with more people.
Nuria:	OK, fine. Where shall we meet?
Carlos:	How about if we meet at the Reina Cristina hotel bar? It's in the centre and, besides, the tapas there are fantastic.
Nuria:	The problem is my moped's bust and it's at the garage.
Carlos:	Can't you go by bus? The number 8 goes right by the door.
Nuria:	No. You always have to wait a lot. My dad will drive me. What time shall we meet?
Carlos:	I've got a football match until 8. Then I have to shower. How about if we meet in the bar at 9.30?
Nuria:	OK. See you later.
Carlos:	Great. See you later.

Answers to questions:
1. She has exams the day after tomorrow and has a lot of work.
2. As she thinks it is going to be really crowded.
3. He says it's more exciting like that.
4. It's very central and the tapas are fantastic.
5. As it's broken.
6. As you always have to wait a long time.
7. Her dad will drive her.
8. Because he is playing football until 8 and then has to shower.

Exercise 6.7

A recording of the completed conversation is available on the CD.

CD 2, track 28

Answers (in bold):

Pedro:	Hola Jorge, ¿qué tal?
Jorge:	Fenomenal. Ayer **fui** al concierto de Ketama.
Pedro:	¡Qué **suerte**! ¿Cómo conseguiste **entradas**?
Jorge:	Mi **amigo** Manolo **conoce** al grupo.
Pedro:	¿**Dónde** tocaron?
Jorge:	En la plaza de toros. Estaba **llena** y había un **ambiente** increíble.
Pedro:	Yo **quiero** ir a la plaza de toros el sábado. Va a haber una **corrida** muy buena.
Jorge:	Yo voy **contigo**, si quieres. ¿Qué toreros van a torear?
Pedro:	El Juli, Fran Rivera y Enrique Ponce.
Jorge:	¿Tú **crees** que va a haber entradas?
Pedro:	No **sé**. Pero mañana voy a la **taquilla** para ver si todavía quedan. ¿Quieres venir **conmigo**?
Jorge:	Vale. Te **llamo** por la mañana para decirte donde **quedamos**.

Translation:

Pedro:	Hi Jorge. How's it going?
Jorge:	Fantastic. Yesterday I went to the Ketama concert.
Pedro:	How lucky. How did you manage to get tickets?
Jorge:	My friend Manolo knows the band.
Pedro:	Where did they play?
Jorge:	At the bullring. It was full and there was an incredible atmosphere.
Pedro:	I want to go to the bullring on Saturday. There is going to be a really good bullfight.
Jorge:	I'll go with you if you like. Which bullfighters are performing?
Pedro:	El Juli, Fran Rivera and Enrique Ponce.
Jorge:	Do you think there will be tickets?
Pedro:	I don't know. But tomorrow I'm going to the ticket-office to see if there any left. Do you want to come with me?
Jorge:	Sure. I'll call you tomorrow to tell you where we should meet.

UNIT 6 | 91

Exercise 6.8
CD 2, track 29

Transcript:

Pedro:	Dígame.
Jorge:	Hola. Soy Jorge.
Pedro:	Hola Jorge, ¿qué pasa?
Jorge:	Pues nada. Te llamo por el tema de los toros del sábado.
Pedro:	Muy bien. ¿Dónde quedamos?
Jorge:	No hace falta porque ya tengo entradas.
Pedro:	¿Cómo dices?
Jorge:	Pues eso, que tengo entradas. Es que mi padre las tenía pero no puede ir.
Pedro:	¡Fantástico! ¿Cuánto cuesta?
Jorge:	Nada. Son gratis, y además tenemos sitio a la sombra. Con el calor que hace estos días no se puede estar al sol.
Pedro:	¡Qué bien! ¿Cuándo empieza la corrida?
Jorge:	Creo que a las siete. ¿Por qué no quedamos a las 6, delante de la taquilla, y así podemos tomarnos un café antes.
Pedro:	Vale. ¿Cómo piensas ir?
Jorge:	Voy andando, ¿y tú?
Pedro:	Voy a coger el autobús. Te veo el sábado.
Jorge:	Vale. Hasta el sábado.

Translation:

Pedro:	Hello.
Jorge:	Hello. It's Jorge.
Pedro:	Hi Jorge. What's up?
Jorge:	Not much. I'm calling about the bullfighting thing on Saturday.
Pedro:	Fine. Where shall we meet?
Jorge:	Well we don't need to any more as I've got some tickets.
Pedro:	What did you say?
Jorge:	Just that, that I've got tickets. My father had some, but can't go.
Pedro:	Fantastic. How much does it cost?
Jorge:	Nothing. It's free, and besides we've got seats in the shade. With the weather being so hot the last few days you can't sit in the sun.
Pedro:	Brilliant. When does the bull fight start?
Jorge:	Seven, I think. Why don't we meet at six in front of the ticket-office and that way we can have a coffee before?
Pedro:	OK. How are you thinking of getting there?
Jorge:	I'll walk, and you?
Pedro:	I'll get the bus. See you on Saturday.
Jorge:	OK. 'Til Saturday.

Answers to questions:
1. *Porque Jorge tiene entradas ya.*
2. *Nada; son gratis.*
3. *Para la sombra.*
4. *A las siete.*
5. *Para tomar un café.*
6. *Jorge va andando/a pie y Pedro va a coger el autobús.*

Exercise 6.9
CD 2, track 30

Transcript:

Carlos:	¿Bueno, niñas, ¿qué hacemos esta noche?
Eva:	A mí, me apetece ir al cine.
Carlos:	Lo que pasa es que yo fui el otro día.
Eva:	Sí, con Nuria, y antes fuiste con Ana.
Nuria:	¿Qué?
Carlos:	Es solamente una amiga.
Nuria:	¿Ah sí?
Carlos:	Sí.
Nuria:	Bueno....Lo siento, Carlos, pero yo también quiero ir al cine. Me gustaría ver la nueva película de Brad Pitt.
Eva:	A mí también. ¡Es tan guapo!
Carlos:	El problema con vosotras es que estáis obsesionadas con los hombres extranjeros. No os dais cuenta de que los hombres españoles somos mucho más guapos.
Eva:	Sois muchas cosas, pero más guapos que Brad Pitt, no.
Carlos:	Bueno, bueno....¿Y cómo se llama esta magnífica película?
Eva:	No me acuerdo.
Nuria:	Ni yo tampoco.
Carlos:	Vaya, vaya...
Eva:	Es que los actores son mucho más importantes que el título.
Carlos:	Pero sabéis dónde la ponen, ¿no?
Eva:	Hombre, claro. La ponen en "Multicines". Me parece que en la sala 5.
Nuria:	No, en la 4. Pasé por allí ayer y lo vi.
Carlos:	¿Y cuándo vamos?
Nuria:	Hay una sesión a las ocho, otra a las diez, y otra a las doce. A mí me da igual.
Carlos:	¿Qué tal si vamos a las diez, así podemos comer algo antes.
Nuria:	Vale.
Eva:	Vale, muy bien. ¿Dónde quedamos?
Carlos:	¿Quedamos en la taquilla del cine y luego podemos decidir adónde vamos?
Eva:	Vale. ¿A qué hora?
Carlos:	¿A las ocho y media?
Eva:	Muy bien.
Nuria:	Estupendo.
Eva:	Una última cosita: ¿Qué valen las entradas?
Carlos:	Cinco euros, pero no te preocupes, os invito yo
Eva:	Muchísimas gracias.
Nuria:	Lo mismo digo, pero, lo siento, Brad Pitt sigue siendo más guapo.

Translation:

Carlos:	Well, girls, what shall we do tonight?
Eva:	I feel like going to the cinema.
Carlos:	The thing is, I went to the cinema the other day.
Eva:	Yes, with Nuria, and before that you went with Ana.
Nuria:	What?
Carlos:	She's just a friend.
Nuria:	Oh yes?
Carlos:	Yes.
Nuría:	Well....I'm sorry, Carlos, but I also want to go to the cinema. I'd like to see the new Brad Pitt film.

Eva:	Me too. He's so good-looking.
Carlos:	The problem with you is that you're obsessed with foreign men. You don't realise that Spanish men are much more good-looking.
Eva:	You're a lot of things, but more good-looking than Brad Pitt, I'm afraid not.
Carlos:	OK, OK…And what's the title of this magnificent film?
Eva:	I don't remember.
Nuria:	Nor do I.
Carlos:	Well, well…
Eva:	The fact is the actors are much more important than the title.
Carlos:	But you do know where it's showing don't you?
Eva:	Of course. It's on at Multicines. I think it's on in screen 5.
Nuria:	No, it's screen 4. I passed by there yesterday and saw it.
Carlos:	What time shall we go?
Nuria:	There's a programme at 8, another at 10, and another at 12. It's all the same to me.
Carlos:	How about if we go at 10 – that way we can have something to eat beforehand.
Nuria:	OK.
Eva:	OK, fine. Where shall we meet?
Carlos:	Shall we meet at the box-office and then we can decide where we go.
Eva:	OK. At what time?
Carlos:	At 8.30.
Eva:	Fine.
Nuria:	Great.
Eva:	One last little thing: how much are the tickets?
Carlos:	5 euros, but don't worry, I'm paying.
Eva:	Thanks a million.
Nuria:	That goes for me too, but, I'm sorry, Brad Pitt's still more good-looking.

Suggestions: The following questions should be asked after the pupils have taken notes:
1. *¿Cómo se llama la película?*
2. *¿Dónde la ponen?*
3. *¿En qué sala la ponen?*
4. *¿A qué sesión van?*
5. *¿Qué valen las entradas?*
6. *¿Qué más información hay?*

Answers to questions:
1. *No se sabe.*
2. *En Multicines.*
3. *En la 4.*
4. *Van a las diez.*
5. *Valen 5 euros.*
6. *Es la nueva película de Brad Pitt; Carlos va a invitar a Eva y Nuria.*

Translations:
1. It is not known.
2. In Multicines.
3. Screen number 4.
4. They're going at 10.
5. They cost 5 euros.
6. It's the new Brad Pitt film; Carlos is going to pay for Eva and Nuria.

Exercise 6.10

Translation of passage:

Dear Elena:

I am writing this letter to you because you do not answer my calls. I am very sad, and I'd like to be able to talk to you. As you know, I'm really sorry about that business in Scotland.

Well, let me tell you a little bit about what I've done recently: the other day I went out with Manolo. We went to the "Ketama" concert. We had a great time. We went on Manolo's motorbike. First, we had some tapas in that bar which you like, next to the bullring. Then we went into the bullring about ten o'clock, but the band didn't start playing until twelve because there were some problems with the sound and they took a long time to resolve it. But it was worth it. How fantastic!

Then, on Saturday, I went to a bullfight with Pedro. It didn't cost me a penny because his dad paid for the tickets. What a piece of luck!

Why don't you tell me what you've done and let's see if we can meet up again.

I really miss you.

Lots of love.

Jorge

Answers to questions:
1. Because she won't answer his calls.
2. They went to a bar to have some tapas.
3. Due to technical problems with the sound.
4. It was free.

Exercise 6.11

Answers (in bold):

Querida Elena:

Te estoy escribiendo esta carta puesto que no contestas mis llamadas. Estoy muy triste y me gustaría poder hablar contigo. Como sabes, siento mucho lo de Escocia.

Bueno, te cuento un poco lo que he hecho últimamente: el otro día **salí** *con Manolo.* **Fuimos** *al concierto de "Ketama". Lo* **pasamos** *bomba.* **Fuimos** *en la moto de Manolo. Primero,* **comimos** *unas tapas en ese bar que a ti te gusta, al lado de la plaza de toros. Luego,* **entramos** *en la plaza, a eso de las diez, pero la banda no* **empezó** *a tocar hasta las doce porque había unos problemas con el sonido y* **tardaron** *mucho en solucionarlos. Pero* **mereció** *la pena. ¡Qué maravilla!*

Luego, el sábado, **fui** *a una corrida con Pedro. No me* **costó** *nada porque mi padre nos* **invitó***. ¡Qué suerte!*

¿Por qué no me cuentas lo que tú has hecho y a ver si podemos vernos otra vez?

Te echo mucho de menos.

Un beso muy fuerte,

Jorge

Suggestions: Either as homework or as a classroom exercise, pupils could be asked to list the infinitives of all the verbs above and then to conjugate them all fully in the preterite tense.

Exercise 6.12

Suggestions: This exercise can be used for homework or, alternatively, as a classroom exercise. If used as the latter, there is clearly scope for oral work in terms of questions and answers.

Exercise 6.13

Suggestions: Before starting this exercise, pupils would need to be taught the following with regard to radical-changing verbs in the preterite: with radical-changing *–ar* and *–er* verbs, there is **no** radical change. However, radical-changing *–ir* verbs **do** change, but only in the 3rd person singular and plural.

Translation of diary entry:
Today I go to the letter-box. I find a letter from *Jorge*. He says he's sorry, but he only talks about himself. He says that he goes out with his friend, that he's having tapas, that he's having a great time. How selfish!

Answers to exercise (in bold):
Hoy **fui** al buzón. **Encontré** una carta de Jorge. Me **pidió** perdón, pero solamente **habló** de sí mismo. **Contó** que **salió** con su amigo, que **comió** tapas, que lo **pasó** bomba. ¡Qué egoísta!

Exercise 6.14

Suggestions: This exercise again provides a good opportunity for oral work in terms of questions and answers.

Exercise 6.15

Answers (in bold):
1. Julio **vio** que su madre estaba enfadada e **hizo** sus deberes muy rápido.
2. Juan **estuvo** en Alemania el año pasado.
3. Ana y Carlos **vieron** una película estupenda el sábado.
4. Nosotros **vimos** a nuestra abuela la semana pasada.
5. Yo **hice** todo lo posible para conseguir entradas.
6. Ella **dijo** que sí.

Suggestions: To reinforce these verbs, pupils should be asked to invent sentences of their own using different parts of the different verbs. This could be done as either classwork or homework. Attention should also be drawn to the *e* in sentence 1.

Exercise 6.16

Answers:
1. *Julio* saw that his mother was angry and did his homework very quickly.
2. *Juan* was in Germany last year.
3. *Ana* and *Carlos* saw a fantastic film on Saturday.
4. We saw our grandmother last week.
5. I did everything possible to get tickets.
6. She said yes.

Exercise 6.17

A recording of the completed passage is available on the CD.

CD 2, track 31
Answers (in bold):
Carlos **hizo** sus deberes lo más rápido posible. **Salió** de su casa a las ocho y **fue** a su bar favorito. Allí **vio** a Ana. Le **preguntó** si quería ir al cine. Ella **dijo** que sí. Carlos **pagó** al camarero y los dos **salieron** del bar y **fueron** directamente al cine. Como Ana no tenía dinero, Carlos la **invitó**. La película **empezó** a las ocho y media y **terminó** a las diez. Después, **cenaron** en un restaurante chino. Carlos **volvió** a casa a las once y media.

Translation:
Carlos did his homework as quickly as possible. He left the house at 8 and went to his favourite bar. There he saw Ana. He asked her if she wanted to go to the cinema. She said yes. Carlos paid the waiter and the two left the bar and went straight to the cinema. As Ana didn't have any money, Carlos paid for her. The film began at 8.30 and finished at 10. Afterwards, they had dinner in a Chinese restaurant. Carlos returned home at 11.30.

Exercise 6.18
CD 2, track 32
Transcript:

Hola. Yo me llamo Julio. Os voy a contar lo que hice en mis vacaciones de Navidad. Fui a Austria con mis padres y mi hermano Paco. No salimos hasta el día 29 de diciembre porque mis abuelos pasaron la Navidad con nosotros y no volvieron a casa hasta el día 28. Fuimos al aeropuerto en taxi y cogimos un avión que salió a las 10 de la mañana. Llegamos a Innsbruck a eso de las 12 y luego fuimos en autocar a la estación de esquí. No me acuerdo exactamente cómo se llamaba, pero sé que está a unas 2 horas de Innsbruck. Al llegar, fuimos directamente al hotel. Subimos a nuestras habitaciones y dejamos las maletas, y luego fuimos a una tienda para alquilar los esquís, los bastones y las botas. Después, sacamos los "forfaits", y volvimos al hotel. Nos cambiamos de ropa y bajamos a las pistas. Empezamos a esquiar a las 3.30 y estuvimos esquiando hasta las 4.30. Después de esquiar, volvimos al hotel y nos duchamos. Luego, salimos y encontramos un magnífico restaurante italiano donde cenamos. De hecho, cenamos allí todas las noches porque la comida era deliciosa.

Esquiamos todos los días menos el miércoles. Aquel día había muchísima niebla, y no salimos del hotel. Jugamos a las cartas y vimos la televisión.

Lo pasamos bomba en Austria. La gente es muy simpática y las pistas de esquí son maravillosas. También, comimos muy, muy bien.

Translation:
Hi. My name's Julio. I'm going to tell you about what I did in my Christmas holidays. I went to Austria with my parents and my brother Paco. We didn't leave until December 29th as my grandparents spent Christmas with us and didn't return home until the 28th. We went to the airport by taxi and caught a plane which left at 10 in the morning. We arrived at Innsbruck at about 12 and then went by coach to the ski resort. I don't remember exactly what it was called, but I know it's 2 hours away from Innsbruck. On arriving, we went straight to the hotel. We went up to our rooms and left our suitcases and then went to a shop to hire skis, sticks and boots. Afterwards, we bought our ski passes, and went back to the hotel. We got changed and went down to the slopes. We started skiing at 3.30 and were skiing until 4.30. After skiing, we went back to the hotel and had a shower. Then, we went out and found a fantastic Italian restaurant where we had dinner. In fact we had dinner there every night as the food was delicious.

We skied every day except Wednesday. That day there was an awful lot of mist, and we didn't leave the hotel. We played cards and watched TV.

We had a great time in Austria. The people are really nice and the ski slopes are fantastic. Also, we ate very, very well.

Suggested questions:
1. ¿Adónde fue Julio y con quién?
2. ¿Cuándo salieron?
3. ¿Por qué no salieron antes?
4. ¿Cómo fueron a la estación de esquí?
5. ¿Cómo se llama la estación?
6. ¿Qué hicieron al llegar?
7. ¿Qué hicieron la primera noche?
8. ¿Qué día no esquiaron y qué hicieron?
9. ¿Qué piensa Julio del viaje y por qué?

Answers to questions:
1. Fue a Austria con sus padres y su hermano.
2. Salieron el día 29 de diciembre.
3. Porque sus abuelos pasaron la Navidad con ellos, y no se fueron hasta el 28.
4. Fueron en taxi, luego cogieron un avión, y, después, un autocar.
5. No se sabe.
6. Fueron al hotel, luego alquilaron esquís, bastones y botas.
7. Cenaron en un magnífico restaurante italiano.
8. El miércoles. Jugaron a las cartas y vieron la televisión.
9. Le gustó mucho. La gente de Austria es muy simpática y las pistas son fantásticas. También, comieron muy bien.

Suggestions: It is worth getting pupils to reply using full sentences, thereby ensuring that they get used to using verbs in the preterite.

Exercise 6.19

Answer to exercise:

Lunes

Me levanté a las ocho. Salí de casa a las nueve y fui al colegio en autobús. En el colegio no hice nada. Terminé a las dos y fui al "Bar Niza". Vi a Ana, y comimos juntos. Yo pedí un bocadillo/bocata de jamón y Ana pidió una ensalada. Hablamos de la película que vimos el otro día y quedamos más tarde para ver una película francesa que ponen en "Multicines". Volví/me fui a casa. Hice mis deberes y luego vi la televisión. Fui al cine y esperé y esperé. No llegó. Creo que piensa que yo salgo con demasiadas chicas.

Suggestions: There is excellent scope for oral work here in terms of questions and answers.

Examples:
¿Cuándo se levantó?
¿Cuándo salió de casa?
¿Qué hizo después de terminar en el colegio?

Pupils should be asked to answer in full sentences and will need to be reminded that they will need to answer using the 3rd person of the preterite as they will be describing what *Carlos* did. In this regard, they should be reminded to listen very carefully to the question, as the correct 3rd person part of the verb will often be supplied in the question. For example, when asked *¿Cuándo se levantó?*, the pupil simply has to repeat *se levantó* followed by the time. Care, of course, needs to be taken with questions that begin *¿Qué hizo......?* As the word *hizo* is extremely unlikely to feature in the answer.

Exercise 6.20

Suggestions: Again, there is good scope for questions and answers here. Individual pupils should be asked to read out their work whilst the others take notes with a view to answering teacher-led questions afterwards.

The verbs in the vocabulary list are *–ar* verbs. Pupils should also be asked to try to use some *–er* and *–ir* verbs. The irregular verb *ir* should also be used.

Exercise 6.21

Answers to exercise (in bold):
1. Yo **hacía** mis deberes cuando sonó el teléfono.
2. Ellos **hablaban** con su abuela todos los domingos.
3. Nosotros **nos acostábamos** tarde todas las noches.
4. **Hacía** mucho calor ese día.
5. Ella **esquiaba** cuando empezó a nevar.

Exercise 6.22

Answers:
1. I was doing my homework when the telephone rang.
2. They talked with their grandmother every Sunday.
3. We went to bed late every night.
4. It was very hot that day.
5. She was skiing when it started to snow.

Suggestions: As well as verifying the answers it is important that the pupils are clear as to why the imperfect has been used in each case. Indeed, in sentences 1 and 5, where the imperfect has been used in conjunction with the preterite, pupils should be made clear as to why one has been used as opposed to the other. This, in turn, may provide scope for them to invent sentences of their own combining the imperfect and preterite.

Exercise 6.23

Answers (in bold):
1. Jorge **comía** cuando **entró** Pedro.
2. Yo **estaba** en Italia cuando Inglaterra **ganó** la copa.
3. Cuando Pepe **salió** del cine, **llovía**.
4. María **hablaba** con su hermana cuando le **picó** un mosquito.
5. Cuando nosotros **fuimos** a la playa **hacía** mucho sol y calor.

Exercise 6.24

Answers:
1. Jorge was eating when Pepe came in.
2. I was in Italy when England won the cup.
3. When Pepe left the cinema it was raining.
4. María was talking to her sister when a mosquito stung her.
5. When we went to the beach it was very sunny and hot.

UNIT 6 | 99

Exercise 6.25
CD 2, track 33

Transcript:

Hola. Soy Pedro. El otro día fui a "La Maestranza" para ver una corrida de toros con mi amigo Jorge. Había muchísima gente en la plaza y cuando salió el primer toro Jorge y yo estábamos muy nerviosos. Hacía mucho calor, pero, menos mal, teníamos sitio a la sombra. Salió El Juli, primero. Llevaba un traje de luces precioso, e hizo una faena muy buena. Luego salió Enrique Ponce, y, después, Fran Rivera. ¡Qué maravilla! Nos encantó. La corrida duró dos horas y media y después fuimos a un bar de tapas, pero había demasiada gente, así que volvimos a la casa de Jorge. Sus padres no estaban, y pasamos toda la noche escuchando música.

Translation:

Hi. I'm Pedro. The other day I went to La Maestranza to see a bullfight with my friend Jorge. There were an awful lot of people in the bullring and when the first bull appeared Jorge and I were very nervous. It was very hot, but, thank goodness, we had seats in the shade. El Juli came out first. He was wearing a beautiful 'suit of lights' and gave an excellent performance. Then Enrique Ponce appeared and afterwards Fran Rivera. It was fantastic! We loved it. The bullfight lasted 2 and a half hours and afterwards we went to a tapas bar, but there were too many people, so we went back to Jorge's house. His parents weren't at home and we spent the whole night listening to music.

Answers to exercise:

Pretérito	imperfecto
Fui	había
Salió	estábamos
Salió	hacía
Hizo	teníamos
Salió	llevaba
Encantó	había
Duró	estaban
Fuimos	
Volvimos	
Pasamos	

Suggestions: There is scope once more for oral work here. After clarifying each individual example of the preterite or imperfect, a question could be asked. For example, after establishing that **fui** is the first use of the preterite, the following question could be asked, *¿Adónde fue Pedro y con quién?* Again, pupils should be encouraged to answer in full sentences.

Furthermore, either as classwork or homework, pupils could be asked to invent their own sentences combining the preterite and some simple forms of the imperfect. Finally, for good measure, and to mark the fact that they have finished the book, they could be asked to translate the passage.